Magic in the Air

Mobile communication
and the transformation of social life

Magic
in the *Air*

James E. Katz

Transaction Publishers
New Brunswick (U.S.A.) and London (U.K.)

Copyright © 2006 by Transaction Publishers, New Brunswick, New Jersey.

All rights reserved under International and Pan-American Copyright Conventions. No part of this book may be reproduced or transmitted in any form or by any means, electronic or mechanical, including photocopy, recording, or any information storage and retrieval system, without prior permission in writing from the publisher. All inquiries should be addressed to Transaction Publishers, Rutgers—The State University, 35 Berrue Circle, Piscataway, New Jersey 08854-8042. www.transactionpub.com

This book is printed on acid-free paper that meets the American National Standard for Permanence of Paper for Printed Library Materials.

Library of Congress Catalog Number: 2006044593
ISBN: 0-7658-0335-6
Printed in the United States of America

Library of Congress Cataloging-in-Publication Data

Katz, James Everett.
    Magic in the air : mobile communication and the transformation of social life / James E. Katz.
        p. cm.
    Includes bibliographical references and index.
    ISBN 0-7658-0335-6 (alk. paper)
    1. Cellular telephones—Social aspects. 2. Telecommunication—Social aspects. I. Title.

HE9713.K38   2006
303.48'33—dc22   2006044593

To Raymond and Frances Katz

I only wish my grandmother had lived long enough to hear the radio. She would have enjoyed it so much."
—Sarah E. Klein, St. Louis, Missouri, June, 1932

Contents

Preface and Acknowledgements

This book presents a series of studies concerning the social settings of mobile communication and information technology. Ethnographic reports, surveys, observation, critical interpretation, and informed conjecture are among the approaches brought to bear on the topic. My predominating theme is how mobile and information technology intersect with long-standing patterns of human behavior and thought, especially in the transcendental and ontological realms.

Information and communication technology is everywhere becoming more prominent, but nowhere more so than in its mobile form. The increasing variety of mobile communication devices are affecting people's lives dramatically, directly, and on a vast scale. As for the mobile phone itself, no technology has ever been adopted so quickly by so many people.

As these technologies have proliferated, a vibrant community of scholars has grown up to investigate them. The emergence of scholars of mobile communication is in stark contrast to the mainstream academic community that has inexplicably ignored the mobile communication revolution. No clearer instance can be seen of this odd situation than in the publication of mainline academic journals such as the *Journal of Communication* (the official journal of the International Communication Association) which in 2005 produced a two-issue set summarizing "the state of the art in communication theory and research." Bafflingly, in none of the manifold articles, including those on feminism, political communication, or communication and technology, was any mention made of mobile communication.

However, the insularity of the traditional scholarly mindset leaves to others a wonderful opportunity. Just as the mobile phone has grown rapidly from a nearly invisible base two decades ago, so too is it the case with the community of mobile communication scholars. When in the early 1990s I began my own research program on mobiles, inspired as I was by the technical breakthroughs of colleagues at Bell Labs and Bell Communications Research, there was little being done in the way of social science research on mobile communication. In some ways, the absence of research was unsurprising because most people had no mobile phones, especially in the U.S. But in another way, it was because millions of people had been using citizen's band (CB) radios and other portable radio devices for decades. So despite the absence of a popular mobile phone per se, there was an already existing extensive trail of human behavior for scholars to analyze.

Another reason the absence of scholarly interest was surprising is in comparison to the fact that there was early and deep scholarly interest devoted to computer-human interaction. In fact, when my Rutgers colleague Mark Aakhus and I launched our Perpetual Contact project in 1999, there was little in the way of empirical mobile phone research or even mobile phone researchers for us to draw upon. Hence we accepted as part of our efforts to study the field the goal of helping to stimulate additional scholarly interest in it.

The situation is dramatically different as the twenty-first century unfolds. Scholarship in both magnitude and insight has continued to grow rapidly. An international community of scholars has blossomed, dedicated to investigating social aspects of mobile communication technology. Scanning the current global scene, one can identify milestone conferences held not only in Budapest, London, and Milan but in Hong Kong, Seoul, and Manila as well. Across the spectrum of disciplines, the social science world seems to be awakening to the interesting questions arising out of the changing way the public communicates, and the research itself is as global as the technology.

The present volume draws on my involvement in this global intellectual enterprise. It provides an opportunity to distill my views about the mobile communication revolution and the social transformations both stimulated by and reflected in it. It is also a continuation of one of the earliest efforts made to survey the consequences of mobile communication. That effort began in 1993. With Philip Aspden, who is now at the National Academy of Sciences, we conducted what seems to be the first national random poll comparing users to non-users of mobile phones in terms of their demographics, attitudes, and behaviors. My earlier book, *Connections: Social and Cultural Studies of the Telephone in American Life* (Transaction Publishers, 1999), presented my analyses of the various aspects of the telephones, both landline and mobile up to the end of the twentieth century. Since that was published, I have been able to investigate a variety of additional topics related to mobile phones; the results of these investigations are presented here. It should be noted that many of the chapters in this volume were published elsewhere in earlier versions and these sources are acknowledged in chapter endnotes.

Scholarship is a communal activity. I have been especially privileged to have had extensive interaction with a community of scholars involved in studies of mobile communication. At the intellectual level, Leopoldina Fortunati has written wisely and well about the subject. At the organizational level, her tireless efforts have helped energize an entire field as she has helped stimulate the development of a community of scholars stretching from the Asia-Pacific rim across Siberia and Europe to North America. Richard S. Ling has also long been a leader in the field. With deftness and subtlety, he has created a masterful set of analyses of how the mobile phone affects life in a variety of domains. He has been an important catalyst for several scholarly initiatives and organizational arrangements, including the Society for the Social Study of Mobile Communication.

Scott Campbell has been delving deeply and profitably into perceptions of the mobile, and expanding further the Apparatgeist concepts proposed by Mark Aakhus and me. Other important thinkers on the subject of mobile communication who have contributed to my views include Naomi Baron, Stefan Bertschi, Jack Bratich, Richard Buttny, Heidi Campbell, John Cary, Akiba Cohen, Ron Day, Jonathan Donner, Nicola M. Döring, Jan Ellis, Mark G. Frank, Laura Forlano, Leslie Haddon, Richard Harper, Joachim Höflich, Hans Geser, Ilpo Koskine, On-Kwok Lai, Patrick Law, Christian Licoppe, Enid Mante, Hartmut Mokros, Raul Pertierra, Howard Rheingold, Harmeet Sawhney, Berit Skog, Lara Srivastava, Edward Tenner, Anthony Townsend, Judy Wajcman, Ran Wei, and Barry Wellman. Each has been extremely helpful in drawing my attention to vital ideas, research and analysis, and engaging me in discussions about the significance of mobile phones.

Over the past several years, the leadership and contributions of Dr. Kristóf Nyíri, both individually and through his conferences based at the Institute for Philosophical Research of the Hungarian Academy of Sciences, has been far-reaching. His work has not only advanced and broadened the field but has also helped create an extensive community among concerned scholars.

Manuel Castells has taken an interest in the field of mobile communication, and already the community of scholars has benefited from this polymath's knowledge as well as his gracious and inclusive intellectual embrace. Ronald E. Rice (now at the University of California, Santa Barbara) and Philip Aspden have provided invaluable intellectual collaborations, including in Ron's case co-authorship of an article upon which chapter 7 is based.

I have been fortunate to have had the opportunity to collaborate with many students. Satomi Sugiyama and Sophia K. Acord have not only helped me identify important studies and analyze data but have also been actively producing their own path-breaking research. As to the present volume, they provided research assistance for chapters 5, 6, and 9. Special thanks is due Yi-Fan Chen for her deep commitment and interest in the field as well as to her assistance at every level. Her tactful engagement of numerous issues has yielded great benefit to the Center for Mobile Communication Studies and to her fellow doctoral candidates. Kalpana David has lent invaluable support and keen insight as the research program of the Rutgers Center for Mobile Communication Studies was established. I also thank students Seong Eun Cho, "Miles" Yoon Whan Cho, Katie Lever, Dan Su, Ferhan Tunagur, and Shenwei Zhao. It has been my pleasure to have worked with these fine students who doubtless will continue to make their marks on the field of communication studies.

In closing, a special note of appreciation is due Dr. Irving Louis Horowitz, Hannah Arendt Distinguished University Professor of Sociology and Political Science at Rutgers University. The university, one of the nation's largest with over 50,000 students, was founded in 1766; Professor Horowitz came to Rutgers University from Washington University in June 1969, bringing Transaction Publishers with him. This means that he has figured (and prominently so) in more than one-seventh of the university's history. Throughout Professor Horowitz's prolific career at Rutgers and Transaction, he has been an intellectual inspiration and a leader in the social sciences. He has also been a fine friend not only to me but also to many others around the world. Yet transcending his manifold achievements in scholarship and publishing is his larger life's work: he has been tireless in his commitment to advancing justice and liberty for all. As he pursued his vision, he has been creating a vastly important intellectual heritage. Thus he helps Rutgers University fulfill the lofty ideal expressed by its motto: *Sol iustitiae nos illustra*—"Sun of righteousness, shine upon us."

Part 1

Mobile Communication
and Social Transformation

1

Introduction

An oft-voiced criticism of modern life is information overload: too much information and too many choices lead to exasperation, depression, or worse. Yet despite complaints, mobile communication technology is being avidly adopted across all demographic segments and social groupings. Mobile devices have become an important way by which people interact with others (as well as avoid doing so). In this process, they are able to gain access to a widening pool of service, information, and entertainment options.

Mobile communication is becoming a way of life, with billions of people expending vast amounts of time and resources via the technology. Statistics from the U.S. concerning mobile phone usage in cars is illustrative of the point. A June 2005 survey of more than 1,200 adults found that 43 percent of all drivers said they had in the prior six months used a cell phone while driving (Roper Center, 2005b). A January 2005 survey, also of about 1,200 respondents, found that 40 percent of drivers said they have talked on their cell phones in stop-and-go traffic to pass the time (Roper Center, 2005a). A still larger study by the U.S. Department of Transportation used direct observation. It found that in 2004 about 8 percent of all drivers during daylight hours were using a mobile device and about 5 percent were using handheld cell phones. These figures translate into 1.3 million and 800,000 motorists respectively. The estimated usage is about double that of 2002 (Glassbrenner, 2005). At the same time, a Harvard University study in 2002 estimated that use of cell phones by U.S. drivers results in 2,600 deaths a year nationwide and 330,000 injuries (Cave, 2005).

Small-scale studies are required to understand the reality of what is going on. Typical of the studies that are needed is one carried out by Rutgers University graduate students Yi-Fan Chen and Katie Lever that has provided a snapshot of mobile device usage patterns. In spring 2005, they observed people, mostly students, at various locations around the Rutgers campus to see how many were using mobile phones or music players (or, in some cases, both). Via systematic (but not random) sampling over several weeks, they eventually recorded 4,500 observations. To say that many young people in the U.S. are now heavily involved with their mobile technology in public places would seem to be an understatement. Chen and Lever found that about 13.6 percent of people were using either a mobile phone or music player, that is, about one out of seven were ambling about on campus with at least some level of involvement with a mobile device. The researchers also found gender differences: of the roughly one out of seven women using mobile devices, three-quarters of them were using mobile phones. About the same proportion of men were using mobile devices, but unlike the women their usage was evenly split between mobile music devices and mobile phones. Based on this study, and one's own casual observation, it does seem that public space is being transformed by individualized, portable information and communication technology. There is also a gender aspect to this behavior. Use of mobile devices for entertainment within one's own world (i.e., music) is more typical of males, while being in communication with others was more typical of females.

There are many places where mobile phones are banned and there are ongoing attempts to impose formal rules as behavioral expectations concerning mobile communication conflict and become redefined. Although these bans are predicated on safety reasons, many in affected areas continue to use their phones while driving. Yet even when safety is not an issue, appropriate mobile communication settings are a frequently contested domain. During a 2004 visit to New York City's Metropolitan Museum of Art, where mobile use is forbidden, I saw young people ducking behind statues to make mobile phone calls, and clerks behind cash registers chatting away. Of course, there is also a distinction between public usage and having a mobile phone on but silent. A sense of just how prevalent "carrying" behavior may be, a 2005 survey of museum goers found that 84 percent of visitors to the New Jersey-area museum were carrying active cell phones into the exhibit area (Goldman and Foutz, 2005).

With about two billion mobile phone users worldwide, and mobile services rapidly proliferating, some intriguing questions can be raised. These include topics of mobile communication in relationship to gender, empowerment, to productivity, socialization and life satisfaction. Mobile communication also problematizes anew significant sociological questions that include cross-group communication and integration, use of public space, sense of time and interpersonal communication and coordination. Not least does mobile communication broaden the range of human possibilities across various levels of human expression ranging from artistic to political. There are also more knotty questions: how do people make meaning out of their technology and how does the technology change humans as individuals and as social participants.

Many of these issues are addressed in the present volume not only in terms of mobile communication, but also, in the book's second part, in terms of telecommunication and information generally. The volume has two major sections. The first section deals specifically with mobile phones and their use, abuse, and social consequences; the second with the social role of telecommunications and information. In order, the chapters address specifically:

1. perspectives on the issue, which is the present chapter;
2. transcendental, religious, and spiritual uses of mobile technology;
3. how "being there" in space and time seems modified due to mobile communication technology;
4. the manner in which mobile communication technology affects self-presentational activities and the choreography of the body in public space;
5. the symbolic inculcation, display, and contested meanings of mobile phones, with special attention to its design and fashion characteristics;
6. the ironies of the way mobile phones have become used in educational settings and their prospects for transforming education; and
7. the way in which crises have become changed due to emergency uses of the telephone. This is demonstrated by an analysis of what transpired during and after the 9/11 terror attack on the U.S.
8. the macro-social role of the telephone as it has evolved since its invention, utilizing a broad-brush perspective;
9. what major ideas have been advanced concerning information societies and their prospects;
10. speculations about the future services that might become available as technology continues to advance, and what some of those social implications might be; and, finally
11. an overview of some enduring issues and concluding remarks.

A thread that connects the chapters is the concern with the social side of information technology, be it mobile or location-bound. On the other hand, the scope of any book has to exclude some material. In the present case, a book devoted to a survey of mobile communication and social aspects of information technology, I have decided to restrict sharply my exploration of other communication technologies, such as television or the Internet even as these are becoming available via mobile phone and other mobile devices.

It is worthwhile making a brief methodological note since I use many different modes of argument and evidence in the book. Some of my claims are based on careful, systematic research that adheres to the stricter cannons of empirical investigation. Other claims are based on a few selected examples uncovered by observers and reporters. Some claims are my own professional judgments. And some of what I offer is pure speculation. I have tried to alert the reader to the distinctions among the various types of claims that are advanced, though in most cases these should be apparent. Certainly it is the case that the better the data are the more one can have confidence in the conclusions that might be drawn from them. I have sought to structure my arguments accordingly. Yet there is also much value in the educated guess or first approximation judgments. This is especially so in terms of setting out questions or issues that can be further explored in a more systematic fashion. Above all, I view human understanding of social phenomena as a dynamic process that invites critical evaluation and ever-improving revision.

The reason I chose the title *Magic in the Air* was because magic is one of the salient characteristics of the technology as it is first experienced by many people. The technology itself not only seems to have a magical feel to it in the way it works but also in the power that it seemingly conveys to the user. Users of advanced mobile devices wander around and yet invisibly connect to just about anyone while accessing information from sources near and far. From an experiential viewpoint, an enormous number of complex functions are crammed into a vanishingly small container. Complex operations can be performed quickly, ranging from calculator functions to geo-position mapping, and from music sharing to making micro-wallet payments at parking meters. For many who have grown up without mobiles, the initial experiences with mobiles can truly seem magical.

Consider a distinction between the practice of magic and the practice of science. Both consist of thoughtways, tools, and procedures. Magic and science have rational ends: the manipulation of the environment to understand cause-and-effect and to produce results. Both are processes and operational systems. But obviously there are some important differences. Science makes universal claims and uses empirically verifiable testing. Magic sometimes makes universalistic claims, sometimes not. However, in terms of verifiable results stemming from magic, there have been none to date. Perhaps surprisingly, there is a substantial amount of money available to anyone who can demonstrate that there is any paranormal, ESP, or other psychic phenomena whatsoever. This includes procedures such as healing touch or psychic surgery, their insurance reimbursability notwithstanding. In point of fact, the James Randi Foundation has had for more than a decade offered a prize of one million dollars "to anyone who can show, under proper observing conditions, evidence of any paranormal, supernatural, or occult power or event" (James Randi Educational Foundation, 2005).

Yet good technology looks like great magic. And as Carl Sagan (1995) pointed out, most people are far more fascinated by pseudoscience, psychics, and the occult than by science. He considers the latter far richer and deeply meaningful, certainly full of surprises. While I agree with his view, I realize that many people do not. Given the proclivity of popular culture and the media that serves it, one should not be entirely surprised that many people take what is essentially a magical approach to mobile communication. So it is entirely fitting that the mobile phone, magical in its appearance, in its operational specifics, and in its power, be accepted by much of the general public as a form of magic. The mobile phone is a form of magic for which someone must pay, generally by subscriberships or prepaid cards. But that is nothing new: anyone who wishes a Tarot Card reading, a papal indulgence, or a curse lifted will find that little in life is free, magical or not.

The title also refers to the too often overlooked spiritual, psychic and religious uses of the mobile phone, an area that has only recently begun to command scholarly interest. This is the topic of the book's keystone chapter. And finally, the title refers to the marketing success of the mobile phone. Contrary to the opinions of many media scholars, this success is a great testimonial not to the magical abilities of copy-writers. Rather it is to the powerful attraction of being able to communicate to others at any time from nearly any place. If nothing else, the success of the mobile phone has been magical, in that in the span of a little more than three decades— from its first experimental use in public in 1973 to the year 2005 – worldwide subscribership has grown to about two billion people. That is, one out of three humans in the entire world has become a mobile phone subscriber. Magic indeed.

Doing magic implies projecting power across geographical space and often in a way that purports to affect the minds of others. Ithiel de Sola Pool (1983) gave wide circulation to the phrase, "technologies of freedom." Certainly the TV and Internet, and even the fax and radio have been given great (and well-deserved) credit for their role in giving the possibility of freedom to people worldwide. Yet it may be that no technology has done more to give individuals freedom than the mobile phone. I say this using the word freedom not only in the political sense, but also in the sense of freedom and control it gives to people over their own personhood. The freedom goes beyond the control of immediate circumstances, such as schedules, contacts with friends, or gaining information access. The importance of mobile communication for advancing freedom for interpersonal relationships of all descriptions has been argued in other contexts (Fortunati, 2003). Of course it cannot be forgotten that power is often reciprocal, and that by definition it means exercising influence over others, and sometimes that targeted "other" is oneself. So while mobile communication can increase one's power and freedom vis-à-vis circumstances and others, it also allows others a degree of control over one.

In 2002, I coined the word "Apparatgeist," to convey a perspective that Mark Aakhus and I were trying to convey in our theoretical approach to the use of mobile communication technology. It combined the sense of "apparatus," or mechanism, with Geist, or spirit. We were not suggesting that inanimate objects have inherent spiritual qualities. Nor did we believe that they could somehow inherit them. Rather, we wanted to emphasize the context-sensitive nature of knowledge and behavior concerning communicative practices, as well as its enduring and transcendental aspects. The emphasis was on the device and the interpretation of the device by its users. The term also was meant to connect the individual and group to show the making of social meaning. We also used the term *Perpetual Contact* to suggest the aim of pure communication that people often strive for, the melding, as it were, of minds. This, of course, is an unattainable ideal, as Peters (1999) has also suggested. (Unbeknownst to us at the time Peters was working in a parallel, albeit more historical, vein.)

For us, though, "Apparatgeist theory" is a lens that attempts to explain communication that is both mediated through personal technologies and also the meaning-making that surrounds the communication device itself. "Apparatgeist" suggests that the physical reality of the machine becomes interpreted in a spiritual light, which then influences both "the designs of the technology as well as the initial and subsequent significance accorded them by users, non-users and anti-users" (Katz and Aakhus, 2002: p. 305). The theory intends to overcome limitations of functionalist and structuration theories by drawing attention to such issues as "the way that people use mobile technologies as tools in their daily life in terms of tool-using behavior and the relationship among technology, body and social role" and "the rhetoric and meaning-making that occur via social interaction among users (and non-users)." It also sought to give a framework for not only the use, but also the non-use, active rejection, and creative reinterpretation of a technology, and thus the material or built order (Katz and Aakhus, 2002: p. 315). In other words, Apparatgeist theory argues that users, non-users and anti-users of technology as well as those who use it in different ways assign different meanings to it. Consequently, it poses a question of "what kinds of meanings are assigned to them by whom."

We argued that greater attention could profitably be devoted to the symbolic and especially affective sides of mobiles. For instance, we urged that spiritual and religious uses of the mobile should be examined more deeply. In part, this book is a limited attempt to help fill in the blank spaces of our understanding of these matters. In particular, we observed the often close emotional attachment that many people give to their mobiles. Although when it comes to the vocabulary of human emotion, it is often hard to distinguish levels of idealism versus materialism, a quote from an interviewee reported by Jane Vincent illustrates the attachment that develops between human and machine: "We'd agreed she'd give her old phones to her younger brother; I found out later that she hadn't been doing

this but had been keeping them under her pillow—the text messages and the calls to boyfriends on these phones were so precious
to her that she couldn't bear to think of her brother using the phones"
(Vincent, 2004).

A further argument was that the mobile phone represented a cul-
mination of a late twentieth, early twenty-first-century zeitgeist or
sprit of the times. Many would say that the mobile phone and, increasingly, mobile entertainment, embodies the zeitgeist of our time;
certainly few technologies are so emblematic of consumption culture to so many the world round. Certainly some advertising themes
suggest that the mobile phone melds symbols of beauty, eroticism,
liberty, and power. Yet, as is clear, there is much more to the mobile
phone than consumption. It is the portable power and connectivity
that it gives to users, enormously magnifying their social reach and
power to alter distant physical circumstances.

Mark Aakhus and I also highlighted what might be considered
non-uses or even "anti-uses." In the case of the anti-users, we found
that mobiles are not simply ignored but rather aggressively rejected.
While there are ever-shrinking numbers of non-users of mobiles,
many continue to say with a quiet pride that they do not want to
become enslaved to a technology, and so refuse to own a mobile.
There are also some who say they make it a practice always to turn
off their mobiles while at dinner. Even ringtones, a multibillion dollar industry, have become engulfed in the meaning-making jostle.
One sociologist told me that she would never have a ringtone based
on music composed by Bach. Doing so would be an "insult" to the
great composer.

There also needs to be a distinction between non-users and users
who use mobile for its impact on those in their immediate surround-
ings, and not necessarily to communicate with distant others. This
distinction may be illustrated by a small study I made in the spring
of 2005. I asked my students about their use of mobile phones for
communicating symbolically with those in the ambient environment
rather than as a tool for transcending space. In discussions with
students I discovered that nearly all of them – twenty-seven out of
twenty-nine—had pretended to be using their cell phones in order
to create an impression on the audience around them. Most of the
students said they had used them for safety (an original motive for
many to get mobile phones in the first place!) and had pretended
that they were in telephonic contact with someone who could help

them immediately (via calling the police, for instance) in case of trouble. As one put it: "When I walk home from the library late at night, I pretend to talk on the cell phone. I do this every time I walk home alone late at night."

Yet there are far more subtle motives and techniques for young people to pretend to be talking on their mobiles. Unpleasant acquaintances can be avoided. Said student "JB," "I was at the student center waiting for a friend and I saw someone really annoying walking towards me. I took out my phone so this person wouldn't do a 'stop n' chat.'" Embarrassing situations can be escaped: student "CL" went into an extremely expensive boutique, not realizing just how expensive it was until she saw the price tags. She was the only client in the store, "and all of the people working there were staring at me. I had no other choice but to pretend someone called me so I could leave the store without feeling like a moron." However, embarrassing situations can also be created by pretending to be on the phone: a girlfriend of "PT" wanted to get her boyfriend jealous so she pretended to talk to her ex-boyfriend. She pretended he was flirting with her. But her boyfriend got suspicious and checked her received calls list—and was able to discover her misrepresentation. As these anecdotes illustrate, there is a large world of communication usage having little to do with those who are distant or virtual and everything to do with those who are co-located, socially and physically with the user.

The mobile phone is quite important to many users, and in my interviews I frequently hear people say, with hyperbole, that if they lost their mobile phone they would die. After all, it contains so much of their lives as well as serving as their phone book, calendar, and clock. In fact, losing one's mobile is in some ways like losing one's mind. Elsewhere (Katz, 2002), I pointed out the almost homunculus-like nature of the mobile. While man may be the measure of all things, the mobile is also the measure of the man, and the woman. This theme is also examined in the chapters ahead, particularly in those chapters analyzing their use in religion, fashion, and identity. Still, a succinct foretaste is in order. An example of the mobile representing the man may be found in a news report from Saudi Arabia worthy of a tale from *1001 Arabian Nights*, a newspaper reported that a young girl in 2005 was able to escape an unwanted marriage proposal. In front of her father, she told the suitor that she would accept his proposal only if his mobile phone was free of unacceptable photos and video clips. Though reluctant, the suitor agreed to the spot inspection. When the photos and videos were seen, there was abundant evidence to reject the potential groom (*Arab News*, 2005).

To understand better the social consequences of mobile communication, in 1996 I proposed a tripartite way to organize analysis of the technology. These are first-, second-, and third-order consequences, a system of division that was adapted from work in the 1960s on large technology systems (Bauer and Gergen, 1968). The first-order consequences are the direct ones: emergency assistance, and social and business coordination. Second-order effects are traceable and not necessarily immediately predictable consequences: SMS (short message service), ringtone customization, geo-locational services. These often develop in surprising ways: emotional investment and seeming addiction, mobile social networks, down-loadable and portable music services, and identity tracking, and location-sensitive commercial promotion. The third-order effects are subtle, and their causal linkages to the technological change are contestable (and sometimes even the existence of the phenomena is disputed). These might include feelings of anomie, stress, irritation, relaxation, depression, or fulfillment. This volume ranges freely across these three levels in an effort to deepen our understanding of, or at least raise significant questions about, the role and effects of mobile communication in our lives. Though far from perfect, the proposed conceptual device may provide a framework that helps organize thinking around the affective and behavioral accompaniments of mobile communication technology.

While I am by no means a technological determinist, I do think that technology is an enabler that opens opportunities and relationships for people. In effect, both the range of human behaviors and technologies get recreated and reconfigured through interaction and recalibration. Most significantly, people seem enormously clever in being able to redirect technology designed for one reason into another direction to serve their inner needs and desires. This reconfiguration process is one of the main themes of the present volume, and is explored in domains from social interaction and spiritualism to education and the nature of the information society.

References

Arab News (2005). Girl rejects marriage proposal. 23 August. Retrieved from http://www.arabnews.com/?page=1&section=0&article=68927&d=23&m=8&y=2005.

Bauer, Raymond and Kenneth Gergen (Eds.) (1968). *The study of policy formation*. New York: The Free Press.

Cave, Damien (2005). Note to drivers: lose the phone (and lipstick). *New York Times*, October 1. Retrieved from http://www.nytimes.com/2005/10/01/nyregion/01cell.html?hp&ex=1128225600&en=48f490f2e6dc906d&ei=5094&partner=homepage.

Fortunati, Leopoldina (2003). The mobile phone and democracy: An ambivalent relationship. In Kristof Nyiri (Ed.), *Mobile democracy: Essays on society, self and politics*. Vienna: Passagen Verlag, pp. 239-58.

Glassbrenner, Donna (2005). Driver cell phone use in 2004. Traffic safety facts. February. DOT HS 809 847. Retrieved from http://www-nrd.nhtsa.dot.gov/pdf/nrd-30/NCSA/RNotes/2005/809847.pdf.

Haley Goldman, K. and Foutz, S. (2005). *Science Now, Science Everywhere front-end report*. Technical report. Annapolis, MD: Institute for Learning Innovation.

James Randi Foundation (2005). One million dollar paranormal challenge. Randi.org. Retrieved from http://www.randi.org/research/

Katz, James E. (Ed.) (2002). *Machines that become us: The social context of personal communication technology*. New Brunswick, NJ: Transaction Publishers.

Pool, Ithiel de Sola (1983). *Technologies of freedom*. Cambridge, MA: Harvard/ Belknap Press.

Roper Center (2005a). Roper Center for Public Opinion Research, University of Connecticut, [USABCWP.021305.R49A]. Retrieved from ipoll database.

Roper Center (2005b). Roper Center for Public Opinion Research, University of Connecticut, USMASOND.05DRIVE.R16G. Retrieved from ipoll electronic database.

Sagan, Carl (1995). *The demon-haunted world: Science as a candle in the dark*. New York: Random House.

Vincent, Jane (2004). Emotion and the mobile phone. Presentation. Retrieved from http://www.surrey.ac.uk/dwrc/Publications/DigiPlay3.PDF.

2

Magic in the Air: Spiritual and Transcendental Aspects of Mobiles

Between Spiritual and Material Worlds

This chapter examines several broad theoretical stances towards technology and social change with an eye towards assessing how accurately they can account for recent developments in mobile communication. In particular, it examines theoretical claims about religious and spiritual uses of technology in light of contemporary mobile communication practices.

As a backdrop, it is worth noting that a permanent fixture of the human imagination is the belief that there is a spiritual world co-existing within, alongside, or just beyond the quotidian world of sensate reality. Many people—in fact, entire civilizations—have shown profound commitment to the primacy of this invisible world. These people also believe that the spiritual world controls the material one. Among the many actions undertaken to assuage or influence this invisible world are charity and the construction of magnificent edifices. But they have also included large-scale human sacrifices and gruesome genocides.

The idea that supernatural forces direct everyday life seems not only an appealing concept but also one that is nearly universal. Paintings in the caves of Lascaux testify to the notion's antiquity, and its appeal today appears no less strong as it animates institution building and daily routines worldwide. Talismanic and magical thinking occurs even when suppressed by other belief systems. Peter Berger has sketched the huge psychological cross-investment in religion due to its importance in organizing human experience, power relationships and institutions:

Religion legitimates social institutions by bestowing upon them an ultimately valid ontological status, that is, by locating them within a sacred and cosmic frame of reference… Institutional order is the reflected or manifested form of the divine cosmos…. The inherently precarious and transitory constructions of human activity are thus given the semblance of ultimate security and permanence. (Berger, 1973: 33)

In contrast to the near-universal dominance of supernatural beliefs, scientific research and technological development (S&T) as social practice arises only in certain cultures and eras. One of the fruits of S&T, of course, has been mobile communication. Mobile communication technology has been made possible only through substantial commitments to research and development. This fact remains true, no matter what the inspiration was for the creative act.

There are many different potential relationships between S&T and spiritualism relative to mobile communication technology. Spiritualism as the term is used here encompasses religion, superstitions, magic, mysticism, and parapsychology. On the other hand, spirituality can be considered a contemplative posture towards or outlook on life, nature, or science itself; as such for present purposes it falls outside the meaning of spiritualism. As is often the case, an analysis such as that undertaken here necessitates committing the sins of both over-simplification and omission.

Perspectives on S&T and Spiritualism

S&T Supersede Spiritualism

One perspective is that S&T, which are natural extensions of rationalism, displace spiritualism, religion, and mysticism. David Hume and Auguste Comte were among the thinkers who anticipated that as S&T progressed, religion would recede. Utilitarian philosopher Jeremy Bentham celebrated technology's role as a moral inspiration. Karl Marx famously called religion the opiate of the masses. Certainly S&T (particularly archaeology, astronomy, and physics) have challenged the status of holy books, including the Bible.

While agreeing that S&T is supplanting spiritualism, a more commonly heard criticism is that rationality and S&T are harming the spiritual side of humanity, a matter of great concern. For instance, the *Lebensphilosophie* (life-philosophy) school of thought, prominent in the nineteenth century, deals harshly with technology. Friedrich Nietzsche, Wilhelm Dilthey, and Henri Bergson, among others, were hostile towards technology and its effects. To them, technology imposed an extreme form of rationality on human existence, limiting or extinguishing its emotional and spiritual sides.

Peter Berger (Berger, 1967) and Gabriel Marcel (Marcel, 1963) are among those who view technology as destroying the transcendent side of life, harming human sensibilities and feeling of existential integration. To them, the spirit of sacredness is fundamentally human, and acts as an important way to make life worthwhile. Peter Berger, even while decrying the situation, sees rationality prevailing over religious legitimations: "for the first time in history, the religious legitimations of the world have lost their plausibility not only for a few intellectuals and other marginal individuals but for broad masses of entire societies" (Berger, 1967: p. 63).

Following this line of thought, there is a more general critique, which could be called the Icarus tragedy. As but one example, Bill Nichols (Nichols, 1988) addresses some themes identified earlier by Walter Benjamin (1936); Nichols highlights occasions when technology has been glorified as holding the promise of ultimate control over destiny. Such a promise is illusory, Nichols argues, and so leads humanity into still greater peril even as simulations of reality replace reality itself.

Nichols' approach is emblematic of a hostility to technology that is prominent in current liberal and leftist academic circles (and which contrasts to earlier eras during which technology was viewed by many brands of Marxists as mankind's salvation). Modern critics devote great effort to showing the moral inferiority of scientific pursuits and repeatedly decry what they see as the morally suspect nature of the enterprise. In particular, they are unhappy with perceived race, class, and gender agendas behind the technical research enterprise. The essence of the intellectual project is to show how technology has been, and is being, used to drive out the meaningful, spiritual and religious side of life.

S&T as a Form of Spiritualism

Other thinkers have emphasized the spiritual nature of scientific pursuits and technological achievement. Oswald Spengler (1932) spoke about technical development as a unique expression of Western or Faustian culture, even as he decried the culture's decline. He saw technology as a unique expression of European dynamism. For Spengler, technology was the spiritual embodiment of the European symbol-soul. Though his thesis has been rejected by professional historians, his leitmotif of decline remains thematically popular.

Lewis Mumford (1946) held that technology, and especially machines, were replacing religion by becoming itself a new religion. Rationality as a central organizing ideology was the result of spiritualism, as embodied in religion, and machines, even though they had often been created to solve religious problems (e.g., mechanical clocks). Mumford saw that machine rationality would destroy magic, since the former could do in actuality what the latter could only pretend to do: to control the natural world and other people.

Jacques Ellul (1964) saw rationality as a way of thinking that drove out other forms of cognition and social interaction. His call echoes that of Weber, and has continued to command widespread interest.

An analysis from the early period of mobile communication, technology noted the importance of the spiritual side of personal communication technology (Katz and Aakhus, 2002). It argued that people invest spiritual meaning and transcendental and collective values into their uses of personal communication technology. Ordinary people do not appear to distinguish between the forces that supposedly act, for instance, when a mirror is broken and bad luck ensues, from those that actually do work, such as when a cordless phone is used. Definitions of science ("using rational means to rational ends") can be juxtaposed with those of magic ("using irrational means to rational ends"). From this point of view, the public does not understand the scientific method or physical laws, so therefore cannot distinguish science from magic.

Davis (1999), for instance, holds that there is little difference between the impulse toward technological control and magic/religion. Spiritual and mystical beliefs are important considerations behind technological innovation. People speak about technology in magical terms, and spiritual perspectives do much to inform the way techno-utopias are constructed. (Here UFO-ology is particularly prominent.) "Magic is technology's unconscious ... our modern technological world is not nature, but augmented nature, super-nature" (Davis, 1999: p. 38). Electricity was initially viewed through alchemistry, being judged as "God's fire" (Davis, 1999: p. 46).

Yet electrical communication technology has also exercised an enormous pull on the transcendental side of the human psyche

(Cooke 2001). Many early experimenters in telecommunications were influenced by its otherworldly possibilities. Jeffrey Sconce, in his analysis of modern electronic communication, noted that these technologies "evoke the supernatural by creating virtual beings that appear to have no physical form" (Sconce, 2000: p. 4). Social scientists were apparently no less likely to be attracted to thinking along these lines. Marshall McLuhan (1994 [1964]) conceived of all media as extensions of our physical bodies and senses. Electricity was related to the nervous system. Since radio's source was invisible, it "evoked archaic tribal ghosts" (404). Radio retribalized us by bringing back aural magic of tribal cultures. McLuhan saw that a breach between people's visual and auditory experiences gives telecommunication technology what appears to be magical properties. Media returns its users to the Word Magic of ancient tribal cultures. But people are either unaware of or deny this effect. For McLuhan, "the universal ignoring of the psychic action of technology bespeaks some inherent function, some essential numbing of consciousness such as occurs under stress and shock conditions" (pp. 406-7).

S&T Used to Pursue Spiritualism

Another argument coalesces around the idea that S&T can be used to advance, prove, or fulfill spiritual ambitions. These impulses seem to be behind the complex geometrical calculations of the ancient pyramid builders no less than cathedral architects. It was no coincidence that the first book published in the West with movable type was Gutenberg's Bible. Sir Isaac Newton spent much of his career in arcane attempts to decode God's divine plan. Many scientists and inventors have been inspired in their work by an attempt to discern or fulfill God's organization or even attempt to contact the spirit world. According to Ronell (1989), spiritual concerns were important background motives for Bell and Watson in their experimental pursuits that led to the telephone.

An extreme formulation may be found in David Noble's work (1997). Noble argues that Western Judeo-Christian culture has become obsessed with technology to an unparalleled degree because technology innately posses a core of religious millenarianism which promises a transcendence of mortal life. By examining the more private musings of the founding figures of modern science and engineering, Noble (like Weber and others before him) shows how technological development was perceived as evidence of progress towards godly perfection. Thus, for Noble (as opposed to Mumford), technology is homologous to religion. Rather than replacing it, technology becomes a way to foster teleological and religious thinking. On a seemingly tenuous basis, he argues that the builders of the great advanced technological systems were seeking to reestablish man's prelapsarian paradise. (The choice of the word "man" used here advisedly). According to Noble, nuclear, genetic, and computer scientists were not aiming in their endeavors to improve society: "On a deeper cultural level these technologies have not met basic human needs because, at bottom, they have never really been about meeting them. They have been aimed rather at the loftier goal of transcending such mortal concerns altogether" (Noble, 1997: pp. 206-7).

Mobile Communication and Spiritual Practices

These issues are obviously multifaceted, but a potentially useful analysis would be to present evidence that religion and spiritualism are of enormous significance to users of mobile communication technology. This may be done by summarizing some ways in which spiritual practices are conducted on mobiles. The evidence consists of providing illustrations of just how active and creative have been the integration of advanced mobile communication technology into spiritualist practices, which include prayer and requests for supernatural intercession, sacrifice, pilgrimage, dress, and socialization. Obviously, this evidence is by no means comprehensive. Nonetheless it suggests that rather than circumscribing, reducing or eliminating spiritualism, mobile communication technology seems to be used to enhance spiritualism.

Religious and Spiritualistic Communication

Although argument by illustration is not a preferred way of proceeding, it may in this situation suffice to suggest how mobile communication technology is used on behalf of spiritual practices. A few instantiations of practices include:

- Conduct of services, including reminding the faithful of the steps in the service, geographical orientation for prayers, and location of worship sites

- Offering and receiving advice, counsel, prayers, and rituals; gathering adherents, recruiting new members, and coordinating the activities of those who are dispersed
- Offerings as gifts to dead and ways to communicate with the dead
- Public display of affect, including religious ringtones and commemorating events
- Commemorating or recording the recently deceased, religious activities, miracles or leaders

Specific examples of these practices include the following. Filipinos, who send about twenty million text messages daily, or perhaps 10 percent of the worldwide volume (*Asian Pacific Post* 2005) are offered a mobile rosary. The messaging service helps the user by providing a visual rosary to follow. This allows the user to count the beads properly, and digitally acknowledge an "Amen" at the right time in the prayer sequence (BBC, 2004). Along the same line, a "Mobile Way of the Cross" leads the subscriber through the prayer sequence without having to physically step through the fourteen stations in a church. A subscription service entitled "Daily Reflections" allows the subscriber to "download and receive reflections and images on different themes from the Mass on that day" (BBC, 2004).

In 2005, the Filipino Catholic Church launched a project that enables Filipinos to have prayers and petitions sent as text messages from their cellular phones to be incorporated into daily masses held in churches in Manila and in the prayers of Carmelite nuns. This is a new service offered by the "Text Mary" project and complements an already-existing service the project offers which is to send a daily prayer via text message. Typical subjects of the prayers are for love and money, finding jobs in Canada, or winning the lottery. The modest cost of each text goes to fund church programs, including a fund for poor families. Project leaders emphasize that the Text Mary project is aimed at offering a handy alternative for those who do not have the time to go to church. A church spokesman stated the project would help Filipinos living at home and abroad, "to reconnect with Our Lord Jesus Christ and Our Blessed Mother, cultivating deep love and devotion to Jesus and Mary." He also said that the Catholic Church wanted to encourage all its priests to use the new medium of evangelization to better reach the Catholic faithful. The project plans soon to expand the services to Filipinos living aboard and add additional mobile features including picture messages, cards, and MMS wallpapers (*Taipei Times,* 2005).

A centuries-old tradition of some Jews is being supplemented by text messaging. Slips of paper containing prayers or requests have for centuries been inserted by Jewish worshippers between the stones of the Western Wall in Jerusalem. Beginning in 2003, an Israeli company will for a fee of about USD 1.20, place in the wall printed SMS-derived text messages. The service seems quite popular, having been used 30,000 times in the first few months of its operation (*Pentacle Magazine*, 2003).

The *Economist* (2005) reports that Irish Jesuits offer a service called Sacred Space, which is accessible via smartphone. It encourages subscribers to spend ten minutes daily reflecting on a specially chosen scripture.

Bella Ellwood-Clayton (2005) reports that among the Filipinos, a typical morning greeting might be something along the lines of "SACRED HEART of JESUS CHRIST shower d person readn dis w ur blessings 2day & always. Gud am!"

Mobile phones have been used to mobilize sect members and recruit new ones. Heidi Campbell reports on evangelical Christians based in the U.K. who have sent missionaries to Ibiza. They use SMS text messaging to coordinate home-based members with their proselytizers "in the field" of Ibiza as they attempt to recruit new adherents. The group apparently finds SMS especially useful to sustain and reinforce religious beliefs among the evangelists operating in the famously decadent nightclub atmosphere of the resort island (Campbell, 2004).

Mobilization occurs in other ways as well. The *Borneo Bulletin* reported that in Brunei, the tiny oil-rich Muslim kingdom, text-messaging has spread outbreaks of hysteria among school pupils during religious studies. Specifically, tales were spread by text-messages that a night-time exorcism would be held at a school. This gossip drew hundreds of spectators to the scene. Local police subsequently responded by admonishing the public that those who spread malicious rumors by text message could be punished (Bendeich, 2005).

As part of the larger picture of using mobile phones to propagate spiritualism, it should be noted that systematic and well-thought out efforts have been devoted to the goal. Sometimes the possibility exists of commercial rewards for successfully achieving this goal even if an important aspect of the process is strengthening religious practices. An interesting case in this regard has arisen with a mobile phone tailored for specific religious practices. In 2004, Ilkone Mobile Telecommunications, based in the United Arab Emirates (UAE), began marketing a device that it claims is "the first fully Islamic mobile phone." (It is branded the Ilkone i800; Ilkone is derived from the Arabic word for universe.) The phone boasts many features that would be helpful to observant Muslims. The GSM-standard phone includes the full text of the Qur'an in Arabic with an English translation, an automatic prayer call (*azan*) with full audio reproduction as well as a silence mode, a prayer alarm before and after *azan*, an automatic direction finding pointer for Mecca directions, a Ramadan calendar and a Hijri calendar converter. According to Saqer Tellawi, CEO of Ilkone, "consumers nowadays view mobile phones as devices which can add value to their self being and inner feelings rather than just a simple communication tool. Ilkone i800 is specially designed to serve Muslims all across the world to address their needs, and add value to their spiritual self being" (Ilkonetel, 2004).

This Ilkone phone not only sends religious texts and messages about when to pray, but also has a special changeover from ring to silent mode when the time to pray occurs.

This helps users avoid a frequent complaint about phones ringing during religious rituals. In fact, ringtone complaints as well as their having grown so loud have caused some Mexican churches to have installed mobile phone jamming devices, preventing signals from getting through. Mosque authorities in Saudi Arabia have installed "a special system which will automatically disconnect mobile phone services when people holding the phone enter a mosque." This measure was taken to avoid disturbing worshippers (Al-Zamie 2001).

Additional variations on religious uses appear to be almost endless. A few more, drawn from the news summaries at the mobile new tracking website *textually.org,* include:

- A Papal Thought of the Day text messaging service is available from the Vatican in Italy.
- To inspire users to contemplate religious matters, the Roman Catholic Church in Holland offers religious ringtones.
- In Sydney, a text message service allows mobile phone users to receive Bible passages directly to their handsets.

Transcendental matters concerning the mobile phone have been taken still further. Uses of it have extended beyond the "spiritual self" and have been applied to spirits themselves. As an illustration, it has become the case that mobile phones are now used as sacrificial gifts and utilities for those beyond the grave. Boxes of sacrificial offerings to the dead, which include items supposedly needed in the afterlife, have been made commercially available in Asian rim countries. Some of these gift boxes include mobile phones; in Hong Kong, for instance, ready-made sacrificial packages are sold that include cardboard mobile phones and pagers (often included among many other luxury simulacra). In Japan, mobile phone antenna dongles and mobile phone toys have been left on religious statues of shrines. In Italy, when a young girl was accidentally killed by Mafiosi, mourners placed mobile phones as memorial offerings on the tombstone.

Thus the mobile phone is taken by many not only as a statement of self, but also as a representative of the self that can transcend states of reality and transmit an expression of will and being beyond the realm of the senses.

Astrology and Fortune Telling

Astrology services are readily available via SMS, and from the number of services and their aggressive promotion, they would seem to be quite successful. Many mobile service providers offer subscriptions to astrology and fortune-telling services. In this regard, a noteworthy program has been developed by TOM, a leading Chinese provider. Genevieve Bell, who conducted a multinational ethnography on behalf of Intel, described a highly popular service in China that offers reports based on the lunar almanac: "Each night you get sent a list of things that are auspicious to do on the next day. This is a traditional activity in Chinese homes" (Bell, 2004).

A variety of interactive astrological services are offered, including interactive readings. One is being operated in conjunction with the National Astronomical Observatories of the Chinese Academy of Sciences.

Spiritual uses appear more than capable of keeping up with mobile communication technology advances. A service advertised through Microsoft Network-MSN offers the ability to "Text a Live Psychic." The ad goes on to say, "In a dilemma? Now you can 'talk' to a psychic by SMS. Text our psychics anywhere, anytime! Just text MSN followed by your question to 86600. Each reply you receive costs £1.50 (O2/Voda/Orange)." But wait, there is more: Russell Grant, a commercially successful U.K. "psychic" offers Astro-Tarot (a combination of astrology and Tarot card readings), MMS I-Ching and rune stone readings. Of the rune stone, Mr. Grant opines, "The MMS Rune Stone Cast—Harnessing the ancient mysteries of the Scandinavian Rune Stone system of divination. Simple and straightforward with true Scandinavian style this service presents the end user with an inspirational daily guidance system" (Mobile services, 2005). The tireless Mr. Grant is also exploring new service offerings and states that he is "presently running trials on streaming content for 3G" that will include video personal horoscopes and Love Tarot cards. (Related to a point made later, in chapter 5, concerning the youthful rebellion and anti-establishment themes often taken in mobile phone ads, it is noteworthy that Mr. Grant's website displays an edgy banner ad for the "Nokia Raw Tour." The Nokia ad promotes rock concerts with "the best breakthrough acts of 2005" and exhorts the reader to "Live Life Loud." Presumably the sentiment expressed in this ad is meant to encourage impolite conduct of oneself in public.)

Unsurprisingly, there is an intersection between affairs of the heart and astrology. Certainly this is the case in terms of romance and partner seeking. For instance, Kalpana David (personal communication) has found that numerous Indian websites offer mobile fortune telling and astrology-based matchmaking.

Mobile Phone Numbers as Magical Power

Interest in numerology is ancient, of course, and as discussed above played a role in the development of S&T. Not surprisingly, the phone numbers and numeric messages are invested by mobile phone users with magical powers.

Agbu (2004) has reported on some Nigerian superstitions and fears surrounding mobile phone numbers. She finds that many people in Nigeria believe that there are demonic or killer numbers. She relates instances in which people are afraid to answer their mobile phones for fear that it is from an evil number. If they mistakenly answer the phone death could result. She says some churches in Lagos warned their followers of the consequences of answering calls of the purported "satanic" numbers. In eastern Nigeria, subscribers "fret over which calls to take and which to ignore, for safety, while many rushed to hospitals to confirm the state of their health, after the news of the killer GSM numbers and deaths." Many think it is "the invasion of the living by the dead and probably a sign of the 'end times'" (Agbu, 2004:17).

She also reports that in 2004, a television commentator told his viewers that

Those who do not believe the existence of the killer numbers run the risk of dying soon. Nigerians should beware of such numbers, but if you must receive all calls, you have to allow the caller to speak first before replying. Once this is done, you are free from the trap. But if you first say hello, you are gone for it (Agbu, 2004: 16).

She also relates the following story:

"a young man in his mid-30s was said to have received a call from a number 017202127. Suddenly, he shouted, 'Blood of Jesus! Blood of Jesus!' before he collapsed." (Agbu, 2004: 16). In some businesses, posted for the benefit of employees is a list of dangerous numbers. One posting warns against answering "any number that ends with 333, 666, 999. They are killing! This is nothing but reality, you are warned! (Agbu, 2004: p. 17)

Not surprisingly, Agbu reports that criminal syndicates use the public's gullibility to defraud those who believe in this process. Sometimes these groups collude to call someone from a "bad" number, and then offer to take away the supposed curse thereby created. She concludes that while there are no physical grounds by which bad numbers can induce death, there are real and painful consequences of these fears among the population. These include the fact that people call less and "a lot of energy is spent brooding over which call to pick and which to ignore" (Agbu, 2004: p. 17).

Dan Su in her research on mobile phones in China (personal communication) found an article in the *Jinghua Daily*, a local newspaper in Beijing, which reported on rental rates for numbers having astrological and homophonic significance. Specifically, numbers can be valued quite differently depending on what the final numerals are. Dan Su found the monthly charges in Chinese yuan (RMB) for numbers ending in 6666 or 9999 were 8,000 yuan, while those ending in 181818 were about 180,000 or more than twenty times as much. The number 888888 went for 1,000,000 yuan. The ending 4 or 7 cost a mere forty yuan. (A yuan equals about twelve cents U.S.)

Numbers 4 and 7 are ill omens in China; the number 4 in Cantonese is a homophone for death. Phone numbers that are incremental, like 1234 or 5678 are expensive as they stand for "making progress." Prices for these numbers are usually up for negotiation. But generally the monthly rent for "good" numbers exceeds 1,000 RMB. For number resellers, there is considerable cross-subsidization of unlucky numbers by those who offer good fortune (Dan Su, personal communication). At the same time, Dan Su has observed that occasionally Chinese nationals who live in the United States have expressed pleasure about the Americans' ignorance of the symbolism of numbers since it allows them to pluck good numbers easily and at no extra cost from domestic providers.

Mobile Phones as Ways to Spiritually Connect

Mobile phones are also used as a way to connect spiritually and symbolically with others who are absent. In Japan, a practice has developed of young people putting photos of their friends on mobile phones. Photos are sometimes affixed to the inside of the clamshell flap, which is considered a privileged position. To facilitate this practice, strategically located in busy arcades are automated photo booths so that people can take snapshots of themselves and turn them into self-adhesive stickers. These stickers are often exchanged among pals as decorations for mobile phones. Yet for some youth, there is an intimate ritual for locating the photo stickers of special friends: it goes on the phone battery's inward facing side (i.e., toward to the phone's body). Such placement provides an emblematically secret, warm place (Satomi Sugiyama, personal communication). While these practices are not necessarily religious, they do reveal how mobiles can serve a highly symbolic albeit non-communicative role in emotional connectedness.

While the notion of mobile phones disturbing funerals is a frequent conversational trope, mobiles are also being used to participate and commemorate the passing of friends and family. One instance may suffice: "Mikko" had recently died. One of Mikko's friends could not attend the wake. So "Anna" used her camera phone to send to a message and image of a burning candle (see figure 2.1) from the wake to the friend who could not attend. (Lighting a candle is a typical way to celebrate deceased people in Finland). The mobile multimedia image-message of a candle substituted for actual

Figure 2.1
Wake Commemoration in Finland via Mobile Phone

attendance. The accompanying text message was, "I lighted a candle. In my thoughts, I am with you remembering Mikko. Anna" (Ilpo Koskine, personal communication, names changed).

Together, these examples show the way in which technology is used to advance and embody spiritual and transcendental aspects of users' emotional lives. In this way, mobiles are a form of affective communication. The examples also suggest the value of a view that sees mobiles as being used in a spiritual way, such as is the case with Apparatgeist Theory. The spiritual uses in more ancillary capacities will be examined next.

Ancillary Mobile Applications

Mobile communication and Internet applications are merging. In this regard, some moblogs (mobile phone blogs or image-based web logs) are used to propagate religious beliefs and images. To some, the mobile phone seems a way to communicate with the dead, a capability that many attributed to the telephone shortly after it was invented. Raul Pertierra reports that communication with the dead is a regular feature of Philippine life and "the cellphone simply provides another opportunity." He related to me that a popular television program in the Philippines, *The Boy Abunda Show,* discussed during one program the cases of three people who claimed to have received text messages from recently deceased friends or relatives. "Upon hearing this, other members of the audience also claimed to have had similar experiences" (Raul Pertierra, personal communication).

Mobiles as Reliquaries

With the enhancement of a camera, the mobile phone can serve as a reliquary or other container of a spiritual or religious experience. For instance, when Pope John Paul II died, many worshippers used their camera phones to take pictures of his photograph on display in churches or on billboards. Likewise, pictures of the recently deceased have been made in areas ranging from Palestine to Finland.

Mobiles are becoming part of religious services. As an example, mobiles have been used to capture the setting sun during pagan solstice ceremonies at Stonehenge. In July 2005, worshippers in the Italian town of Acerra claimed they saw a statue of the Virgin Mary move her legs. The local church was flooded with visitors who came "armed with mobile phones in the hopes of filming a statue of the Virgin Mary that residents say has miraculously moved her legs." Monsignor Antonio Riboldi, the bishop emeritus of Acerra, was skeptical: "In the past, the Madonna has made apparitions in a field or in a cave, but she has never appeared on a mobile phone or a video camera. She doesn't tend to make a spectacle of herself" (Reuters, 2005).

Blessing Phones

Taiwanese interest in Matsu, the popular Chinese goddess of the sea, has been tapped by a company that has manufactured a special Matsu mobile phone, complete with a hologram of the goddess, ring-tones featuring religious chants, and Matsu wallpaper for the display pad. Most relevant is that all the phones have been blessed in a ritual at a Matsu temple (Textually.org, 2004), and can download special Matsu music from the web. Originally only 2,000 phones were made (each selling for about USD 300); however the demand was so overwhelming that an additional 1,000 were produced before the run was permanently ended (Yi-Fan Chen, personal communication).

In the course of her work, Genevieve Bell met women in southern China who had their mobiles blessed by Buddhist monks. They did this, she reports, because the women wore the mobiles close to their chests daily, and they believed that the blessing would prevent the purported evil spirits associated with the phone from harming them (Bell, 2004).

Sorcery

The belief in evil spiritualism being spread via mobile phones or being discharged from them is not limited to China, by any means. There are also reports of mobile phones being used for sorcery and emanating evil. For instance, a news report from Saudi Arabia in 2004 says that the head of the country's Committee for Psychological Welfare, a branch of the government's charity for social services, warned that mobile phone cameras were being used for black magic and sorcery (*Arab News*, 2004a).

Connecting to Afterlife

Mobile phones are also used analogously for transportation into the next world. This impulse is comparable to ancient Egyptian and current East Asian practices of including tokens with the deceased. These may be for either tangible or symbolic reasons, or even status motives. Sometimes mobile phones are left at gravesites as tokens of remembrance. They are also included in the casket with the deceased. Coffins shaped like mobile phones are sold in Ghana.

Tokens

Laura Forlano (personal communication) has documented a practice in Japan of hanging mobile phone antenna dongles on Jizou statues in shrines. The Jizou statues are placed at shrines in Japan to commemorate children unborn due to abortion or miscarriage. It was unclear as to precisely why they were placed on the statues, but they did seem to be part of a religious ritual, perhaps of ablution, at the nexus of private and public symbolism.

Switching from the details of usage, the next section examines the religious contexts and larger social setting in which mobile technology is located. In particular, the way in which ostensibly conservative religious groups adopt the technology is contrasted with some of the ways in which mobiles are used to subvert the social order as religious authorities would like to have it.

Conservative Religious Values and Mobile Phone Use

Howard Rheingold notes that even though the Amish are extremely conservative, the cell phone has been widely adopted among them (Rheingold, 1999). Some have even claimed that the cell phone is widespread among Amish youth. There would indeed seem to be few exceptions among the many religious groups who reject modern garb, and most aspects of modern life, but readily embrace mobile communication technology. It is interesting to consider the logic that allows religious authorities to permit one form of modernism, but reject another.

Until 2005, the camera phone was officially banned in Saudi Arabia for religious reasons. Even during the ban, though, they were sold widely: "The phones are on sale and advertised. The fact that they are in the Kingdom in sufficiently large quantity as to be on sale in almost every store indicates they are being imported in bulk" (Mishkhas, 2004). In particular, there had been and continues to be conservative opposition to the corrosive influences of human images, particularly those of women. This may be highlighted by two press reports. In 2003, a cell phone camera sparked a fistfight at a women's party, and police had to be called to intervene. At a women-only wedding celebration, an uninvited guest was caught snapping pictures of other women and sending them to her boyfriend. In the words of one attendee, "She took a picture of one lady and immediately sent it to her boyfriend, who happened to be the brother of the lady in the photograph. As soon as he received the photo on his mobile, he called his sister and told her what was going on." The culprits were located by the sister and her party, who destroyed the cell phone, and a fistfight ensued (Fareed, 2003).

In a second incident, a Saudi tribe fined the father of a girl who was caught taking photos with her mobile phone camera during a wedding. (The fine would go to a tribal fund for assisting young men in the tribe to get married.) (*Arab News*, 2005).

Despite the camera aspect leading to mobile phones being restricted among some religious communities, the mobile phone itself is used heavily among many orthodox religious populations, including those in Saudi Arabia.

> Although widely used across the country, camera phones are illegal in the Kingdom. In many cases the phones have been used to invade privacy, particularly of women, prompting fights at markets, wedding halls, schools and other public places as well as triggering family disputes…. Body search is a common practice in universities for all female students to ensure they don't carry camera phones. Girls, however, find ways to hide the devices and bring them to lecture rooms. In wedding halls, some operators have resorted to hiring special search squads to check every invitee to ensure they leave their camera phones out of the hall. (Harrison, 2005)

A phone designed especially to assist Muslims in practicing their faith was mentioned above. Similar impulses to use communication technology in religiously supportive ways have been introduced in other faith communities. To illustrate, an Israeli mobile company introduced a handset and phone service to cater to the million-strong ultra-Orthodox Jewish community residents there. It had the phone certified and stamped as "kosher" (MacKinnon, 2005). The discrete black phone is essentially a Motorola handset, but advanced services, such as Internet access, SMS text services and video and voice-mail applications, are disabled. This new phone was born out of concern that new mobile services could erode ultra-Orthodox values and way of life, particularly among the young.

Speaking more generally, it is interesting to note that mobile phones seem to have been quickly adopted by religious leaders. They are also easily integrated into special costumes required by various religious groups. I have observed, for instance, on several occasions, Muslim women using their headscarves as a way of holding their hand-held style mobile phones against their ear and cheek, thus turning them effectively into a headset. This novel melding of ancient and contemporary highlights the flexibility with which the mobile phone has been integrated by those who otherwise hew to traditional lifestyles. Priests of various religious orders, while often forsaking contemporary affordances and costume enhancements, commonly adopt the mobile phone. They can be seen, for instance, dangling from a lanyard or belt, often located next to a religious symbol.

Mobile Communication and Phones as Corrosive to Religious Practice

Just as mobile communication has been used to ease and propagate the spread of religious beliefs, the technology has also been used to escape the more rigorous requirements of religious practice. This in turn leads religious authorities to take countermeasures. To illustrate, bishops in the Philippines have ended a program that allowed people to attend confession and receive absolution via text messages (*Economist*, 2005). (The relationship between the recently ended program and the mobile religious assistance described above remains unclear.)

The bans on images from some religious authorities are clear. For instance, Jeddah's grand mufti, Sheikh Abdul Aziz Al-Asheikh, went to the trouble of condemning as un-Islamic trading in camera-equipped mobile phones since they can take what was described as "illicit" pictures, according to press reports, since they could "spread vice in the community" (*Arab News*, 2004b).

Despite bans on some cell phone uses by religious authorities in Saudi Arabia and the Philippines, as seen above, other ways are also encouraged by authorities in these countries. But use of cell phones in an innovative and perhaps humorous way, has even led to threats of bodily injury and substantial fines when one group is perceived to be incorporating cell phones in objects that offend another group. This occurred in Malaysia in 2003 where statues had been introduced of the elephant-headed Hindu god, Lord Ganesh, holding a mobile phone in one of many arms. The Hindu community there greeted the introduction with outrage, and the government stepped in to forbid sales of the offending statues. Fines were threatened to any vendor who displayed the item (*Agence France-Presse, 2003)*.

Not all spiritual services for mobile communication are altruistically motivated. They can be used with malice aforethought for exploiting the gullible. As but one instance, Finnish authorities closed a service that had been offering SMS messages that were supposedly from Jesus to the subscriber. The cost was Euro 1.20 for each message (*Economist*, 2005).

Finally in this regard, it is worth noting that although the possibility was investigated nothing significant was found in terms of using mobile phone technology to advance secularism and rationality as a belief set. (Of course, this does not mean that they do not exist, only that they do not seem very prominent in the literature.) Such activities would have reasonably been expected had the theories of rationalism superseding spiritualism or of technology draining life of its meaning been correct in this domain. Mobile communication technology does not seem to be a direct corrosive of spiritual life.

Mobile Technology Extends Rather Than Blunts or Replaces Spiritualism

Taken as a whole, mobile communication technology appears to have been widely adopted and heavily used in many places around the world to pursue and promote spiritual matters. While social and business uses have been enormous, by contrast, there is no concomitant use among mobile phone users for rationality-promoting behaviors. Neither does much appear to have been done to propagate secular or rational worldviews via advanced mobile communication technology. (I have also noted a parallel absence of uses to advance public education in chapter 6.) If people did use mobile communication technology for expanding and enriching or even propagating their spiritual views, then that would constitute evidence for the "subjugation" or "superseding" perspectives of S&T's impact on spiritualism. But that is not the case. So absent data, these perspectives appear incorrect.

There is an irony here: only empirical analysis and experimentation has enabled the creation of mobile communication systems. The system's continuing proliferation could only have been accomplished through the application of rational, analytic tools. Yet the necessity of these tools for creation does not mean that somehow their conceptual templates are carried forward to, much less adopted by, the system's users. So despite occasional claims, there is as yet no reasonable evidence that supernatural invocation or messages from beyond were responsible for the technical breakthroughs that have allowed for the creation of the many complicated and interlinked technologies of today's communication system.

The case seems to be that people use their tools to advance and explore their interests and proclivities. There is a long-standing concern over the spiritual side of life, and technology has at various times been used to help in the pursuit of this concern, including by many people nowadays. Recognition of this fact helped inspire Apparatgeist theory (Katz and Aakhus, 2002), and the analyses contained in the edited volume, *Machines that Become Us* (Katz, 2003*)*. Such theories predict that personal ITCs would be increasingly embraced as spiritual emissaries and even imputed to have spiritual powers themselves. Thus, in a paradoxical way, technology is used for the pursuit of anti-technology or more accurately technology is seldom pursued for its own sake but rather for what it can do or bequeath upon the user.

Various psychological studies have shown how people impute meaningful messages from randomly generated phenomena. This generalized aspect of the human brain has been particularized many times when researchers had specific interactions with new technologies that greatly increased human powers of communication and observation. Peering through early microscopes, a scientist thought he spotted miniature humans within sperm cells; deploying newly improved telescopes, astronomers thought they could see canals on mars. Some of those early radio listeners who heard strange noise felt certain they were hearing signals from intelligent beings on distant planets or the ethereal chatter of heavenly souls. From my viewpoint, a great paradox is that so many people embrace fervently technology to communicate with seemingly distant supernatural worlds. In reality they are only communicating with an echo of their own limited selves.

Note

This chapter is based on, Magic in the air. Conference presentation, Hungarian National Academy of Sciences, Budapest, April 29, 2005.

References

Agence France-Presse (2003). Hindu idol with mobile phone provokes uproar in Malaysia. *Agence France-Presse*. September 25, 5:27 AM ET. Retrieved from *http://www.network54.com/Forum/thread?forumid=186926&messageid=1064497632&lp=1064497632.*

Agbu, Jane-Frances (2004). From 'Koro' to GSM 'Killer Calls' scare in Nigeria: A psychological view. CODESRIA Bulletin (Council for the Development of Social Science in Africa), 3 & 4, pp. 16-19. Retrieved from *www.codesria.org/Links/Publications/bulletin3_04/agbu.pdf.*

Al-Zamie, Abdul Kareem (2001). System to cut mobiles in mosques. *Arab News*, August 10. Retrieved from *http://www.arabnews.com?page=1&section=0&article=4625&d=10&m=8&y=2001.*

Asian Pacific Post (2005). Filipinos pray for love. Asianpacificicpost.com. Retrieved from http:// www.asianpacificpost.com/news/article/667.html.

Arab News (2004a). Mobile phone being used for sorcery. *Arab News*, August 12. Retrieved from *http://www.arabnews.com/?page=1&section=0&article=49721&d=12&m=8&y=2004*

Arab News (2004b). Grand Mufti slams trading in camera cell phones. *Arab News*, September 30. Retrieved from *http://www.arabnews.com ?page=1&section=0&article=52164&d=30&m=9&y=2004.*

Arab News (2005). Tribal punishment for wedding snapper. *Arab News*, August 21. Retrieved from *http://www.arabnews.com/?page=1&section=0&article=68783&d=21&m=8&y=2005.*

BBC (2004). Asia puts faith in mobiles. BBC Online, April 28, 08:08 GMT 09:08 UK. Retrieved from http://news.bbc.co.uk/1/hi/technology/3663283.stm.

Bell, Genevieve (2004). Insights into Asia: The digital home, mobile technologies, and technology usage models. *Technology@Intel Magazine*, July 2004. Retrieved from *http://www.intel.com/ technology/techresearch/reallives.htm.*

Bendeich, Mark (2005). Putting SMS genie back in bottle (Reuters). *Hindustan Times*, September 2. Retrieved from ttp://www.hindustantimes.com/news/181_1479540,00040006.htm

Benjamin, Walter (1936). Excerpts, *The work of art in the age of mechanical reproduction*. Retrieved from http://www.marxists.org/reference/subject/philosophy/works/ge/ benjamin.htm.

Berger, Peter L. (1967). *The sacred canopy*. Garden City: Doubleday, 1967.

Campbell, Heidi (2004). "This Is My Church": Seeing the Internet and Club Culture as Spiritual Spaces. In Dawson, Lorne L. and Douglas E. Cowan (Eds.), *Religion online: finding faith on the Internet*. New York: Routledge, pp. 107-121.

Cooke, Andrew (2001). *Electroplasm: Technology's indissoluble link to the spirit world*. [Masters Dissertation]. Royal College of Art, London. Retrieved from *http:// www.interaction.rca.ac.uk/alumni/00-02/andy/plasmic-city.htm#_ftn31.*

Davis, Erik (1999). *TechGnosis: Myth, magic, and mysticism in the age of information*. New York: Three Rivers.

Economist (2005). "A spiritual connection," *The Economist* 374 (March 12), Issue 8417, Special Section p12, 2p, 2c.

Ellul, Jacques (1964). *The technological society*. New York: Vintage.

Ellwood-Clayton, Bella (2005). Texting and God: The Lord is my Textmate, folk Catholicism in the cyber Philippines. In Kristof Nyiri (Ed.) *A sense of place*. Vienna: Passagen Verlag, pp. 91-106.

Fareed, Saleh (2003). Cell camera sparks fistfight at women's party. *Arab News*, January 04. Retrieved from *http://www.arabnews.com/?page=1&section=0&article=21681&d=4&m=1&y=2003*

Harrison, Roger (2004). Camera phones freely available despite ban. *Arab News*, April 04. Retrieved from http://www.arabnews.com/?page=1&section=0&article=42472&d=4&m=4&y=2004.

Katz, James E. (Ed.) (2003). *Machines that become us: The social context of personal communication technology*. New Brunswick, NJ: Transaction Publishers.

Katz, James E. and Mark Aakhus (Eds.) 2002. *Perpetual contact: Mobile communication, private talk, public performance*. Cambridge: Cambridge University Press.

MacKinnon, Ian (2005). Kosher phone taps into new market for mobiles. *The Times of London*, March 03. Retrieved from http://www.timesonline.co.uk/article/0,,251-1508115,00.html.

Marcel, Gabriel (1963). *The existential background of human destiny*. Cambridge, MA: Harvard University Press.

McLuhan, Marshall (1994 [1964]). *Understanding media: The extensions of man*. Cambridge, MA: MIT Press.

Mishkhas, Abeer (2004). Saudi Arabia to overturn ban on camera phones. *Arab News*, December 17. Retrieved from http://www.arabnews.com/?page=1&section=0&article=56187&d=17&m=12&y=2004

Mobile Services (2005). Text a psychic & answer those burning questions on the move. Retrieved from http://www.live-astro.com/mobile.

Mumford, Lewis (1946). *Technics and civilization*. New York: Harcourt Brace.

Nichols, Bill (1988). The work of culture in the age of cybernetic systems. *Screen 29*, no.2 winter, pp.22-46.

Noble, David F. (1997). *The religion of technology, the divinity of man and the spirit of invention*. New York: Alfred A. Knopf.

Oswald, Spengler (1932). *Man and technics*. New York: New York: Alfred A. Knopf.

Pentacle Magazine (2003). Israelis send text prayers to Western Wall. *Pentacle Magazine* Website, September 26. Retrieved from http://www.pentaclemagazine.org/pn760/index.php?name=News&file=article&sid=994&theme=Printer.

Rheingold, Howard (1999). Look who's talking. *Wired 7.01*. January. Retrieved from http://64.233.161.104/search?q=cache:5g25AbmbfJAJ:www.wired.com/wired/archive/7.01/amish.html+amish+cell+phones&hl=en.

Reuters (2005). Pilgrims leg it to Acerra. Reuters July 26, 1:17 PM ET. Retrieved from http://www.smh.com.au/news/unusual-tales/global-village/2005/07/29/1122144022426.html.

Ronell, Avital (1989). *The telephone book: Technology, schizophrenia, electric speech*. Lincoln: University of Nebraska Press.

Sconce, Jeffrey (2000). *Haunted media: Electronic presence from telegraphy to television*. Durham, NC: Duke University Press.

Taipei Times (2005). Filipinos pray for love, money via SMS. *Taipei Times*, August 31. Retrieved from *http://www.taipeitimes.com/News/world/archives/2005/08/31/2003269834*

Textually.org (2004). Texting faith. August 24. Retrieved from *www.textually.org/textually/archives/2004/08/005045.htm*.

3

A Nation of Ghosts? Choreography of Mobile Communication in Public Spaces

In the more than three decades since its first public demonstration in 1973, the mobile phone has grown to command a huge and growing presence in the lives of billions of people. Doubtless the technology has been an enormous success, much desired and much used. Cell phones and other personal communication technologies continue to be embraced by people across the entire social spectrum, so much so that their popularity has far surpassed that even of television (Katz, 2003).

The phenomenon of mobile phone use and the effects of that use, are of growing interest to scholars, and a rapidly growing literature has been focusing on the questions of social management of mobile processes (Fortunati, 2002; Ling, 2004; Rice, 1999). Naturally enough, these studies often target the unusual, the ethno-methodological, and the normative aspects of this technology. Too, when one considers the folk discussions as reflected in casual conversation, editorial pages of newspapers, and chitchat at social gatherings, one also picks up a sense of unease about what these devices are not only doing for us but also to us (Gergen, 2003; Sugiyama and Katz, 2003).

Disturbances to Ordinary Communication Choreography

Undergirding much of the discussion, however, is the often tacit question of whether the social and phenomenological disequilibria that mobile communication set in motion are in their very essence transient and epiphenomenal, or rather profoundly at odds with human nature. That is, on the one hand, one sees that people are everywhere using and enjoying their mobile phones. And, on the other, one hears everywhere people complaining about the irritation they experience when others use these technologies (Fortunati, 2003; Ling, 2003; Rice and Katz, 2003).

One way this topic could be explored is in terms of whether these disturbances are normative, and thus likely to disappear, or inherent in the nature of the way one operates as a human (Rice, 1987). To put the matter prosaically, is the irritation and displeasure that result from the public use of mobile phones comparable to ethics, politics, or fashion, all of which can change rather quickly, or biology, which changes but little over many generations?

Examples may serve to illustrate the point: various cultures find a political regime (e.g., socialism) or a pattern of men's facial hair (e.g., goatees) odious at one time and attractive at others. People often apprehend phenomena that in prospect seem plastic and tractable but prove ultimately to be intransigent, such as listening attentively to two conversations at the same time or going without sleep indefinitely. Both of these tasks seem plausible, but despite repeated attempts, they turn out to be beyond human capability.

When it comes to mobile communication, a legitimate question may be raised as to whether humans are hardwired in a way against being comfortable with mobile phone use by others when they share public space with them. Many experts assert that the irritation people experience from public use of mobiles is a matter of acclimatization and thus is transient: with exposure comes equanimity. This may indeed be the case. But it may not be the case. I think there are some good reasons that humans are likely to continue to be at least partially unhappy with the public use of the mobile phone, and I would like to investigate some of those reasons here.

I explore this question drawing on several disciplines. The primary one, though, is social psychology. Yet, as I hope to demonstrate, the investigation of this topic is wide ranging, and cuts into areas that as far as I can tell have been little explored in terms of some of the enduring issues about public use of mobile communication.

Defining Hardwired

Before delving further into the possibility that people will be permanently irritated by the process of public mobile communication,

it is necessary for me to address the concerns strict social construc-
tionists would have, for they deny that there is much if anything
that could be plausibly hardwired (Clark and Grunstei, 2000). I address these concerns so that those who hew to a heavily environmental viewpoint in the "nature versus nurture" debate do not dis-
miss out of hand my entire intellectual enterprise even as I seek to
unfold it. For those who are stalwart in rejecting the usefulness of
the term hardwired in its more far-reaching sense, please substitute
the phrase "strongly conditioned by our culture." If you do not accept the notion that people are behaviorally conditioned, I would
suggest that you use the term "enduring artifact of our socially constructed culture." However, the point here is less the source of these
potentially invariant aspects of human nature than it is the degree to
which the public use of mobile phones runs up against some invariant dimension of humans. (In terms of the question of which of
these worldviews are most usefully applied to the domain that contains the problem, my view is pragmatic: there are a variety of lenses
that can be of greater or lesser use in understanding the phenomena
under consideration.)

To begin, an explanation of what I mean by hardwired is in order. By this term, I assert that people have ingrained predispositions
to act in certain ways. Following Stephen Jay Gould (Gould, 1995),
I would claim that these ingrained predispositions generally have
the consequence of often (but not necessarily) helping a species
survive, that is, people and all other living organisms have "the
selfish gene" (Dawkins, 1976). Having said this, I do not claim that
humans are micro-genetically driven, that is, have a gene for every
specific trait (Pinker, 2002).

Moreover, this is not the same as asserting that humans have no
choice in the matter. I think the situation is analogous to food. All
people must have at least a modicum of interest in food, and doubtless are genetically programmed to want it. Yet there is tremendous
variety in what people enjoy eating, how much they eat, and what
they avoid eating. Genetic programming can in times of abundance
be quite dysfunctional and lead us to overeat, and to an early death,
hardly the recipe, as it were, for survival! And, despite the fact that
people are genetically programmed to eat, it is possible for people to
decide they do not wish any longer to eat, and starve themselves to
death. In the cases of protests, this could be interpreted as demon-
strating the triumph of willpower over biological dictates (Shell, 2002).

Therefore, in some sense those who hope that we might "get over" our obsession with food are fighting an uphill battle. Too, those who might wish to restrict the public sale of food are also unlikely to succeed over the long haul. This brings me back to the focus of inquiry, namely the possibility that it is inherently pleasur- able to contact others in one's circle using mobile phones, including and perhaps even especially in public places, but equally it is irritating for one to be around strangers who are using their mobile communication devices in public places.

The Presence of Others

As to the first of these processes—the pleasure of our communication activities—it seems very much the case that humans are hardwired to seek social contact. Left to their own devices (forgive the double entendre), people will be inclined to find others with whom they can communicate, that is, people will seek Perpetual Contact (Katz and Aakhus, 2002). (The term Perpetual Contact is, as mentioned in the book's introduction, the title colleague Mark Aakhus and I chose for our edited book surveying the worldwide consequences of the mobile phone. This term implies that contact with others is the homeostatic situation many prefer.) Of course, this is an impulse that varies in degree from person to person, and is possible to resist. Nevertheless, it is common enough to be characterized as a human trait. It is noteworthy that even the definition of introvert connotes a preference for a few close and intense communication encounters over many superficial ones, rather than a preference for no contacts whatsoever.

The reasons for this preference for contact would seem apparent. Using communication skills, humans are able to organize individual resources into a collective that can turn a mammoth into dinner or send an astronaut to the moon. Further, the prolonged helplessness of infants is easily discernable, and the infant learns or is programmed to present numerous communication strategies with which to engage an adult's attention. These include the coo and the smile. Clearly, there is a reason why a baby's scream is so hard to ignore.

According to child psychologist Esther Cohen (personal communication), it is a fairly common phenomenon for infants and toddlers try to open the eyes of their sleeping parents. I think that most of us are able to confirm directly or indirectly the validity of her observation. She suggests that children have much difficulty separating physical presence and emotional presence, so that when parents are present with their eyes shut, and are not responsive to their kids, the kids can feel distress with this imbalance. Hence the best and easiest way for them is to try to pry open the eyes of the parents, assuming that eye contact will bridge the gap between the physical and the emotional presence. This will reestablish the normal situation, namely that the parents are alert and able to interact with (and thus protect) the child.

This same situation makes it hard for homebound spouses of telecommuters to ignore the fact the telecommuter is in a state of "absent presence." They continually find reasons to interact with the spouse, and often find it difficult to accept the fact that even though the telecommuter is physically present, the expectation is that the telecommuter should be unavailable. (Certainly, the similar problem of ignoring someone who is present works in the opposite direction as well.)

So drawing on these examples, several reasons could account for why people will have continuing difficulties with the use by others of mobile phones in public: such use cuts against deeply ingrained patterns of behavior.

In-Group versus Out-Group Communication Choreography

A second trait is that humans are in-group/out-group sensitive (often referred to as the "social identity" approach). One likes people who are part of one's own group, and tends not to like people who are members of the out-group. This holds true regardless of the distinguishing trait. This phenomenon can be readily observed in daily life. Young people join one or another fraternity and feel loyalty to members of their own "superior" fraternity, and are competitive with the "inferior" members of other fraternities. This robust finding is readily reproduced in the social psychological laboratory. For instance, Tajfel and Turner (1979) have shown the following: upon completing a non-meaningful task, subjects are randomly informed that they belong to one group as opposed to another (e.g., "high estimators" versus "low estimators" of the number of dots on a sheet filled with dots). Bonds quickly form among those who belong to one arbitrary group, and the members of any given group soon begin commenting about the ways they are superior to the other group. Loyalty, pride, and esprit-de-corps grow within the membership of one group, but boundaries arise against outsiders and the outsiders, who begin to be seen in less favorable terms. (Again, I am speaking in generalities, and readily admit to occasional exceptions to these social processes.)

The territoriality issue must also be considered. People are sensitive about their immediate space (as Edward Hall has shown in his classic work). Interestingly, some observational research has been done about the use of public pay phones in public space. This research has demonstrated that people will talk longer on the public phone if someone is waiting to use the phone. That is, people defend what was public space, holding it as their own territory, if it appears it will be invaded or used by someone else. (Similar results have been shown with parking spaces: individuals leaving a parking space will take significantly longer to depart if someone else is waiting to take the space.)

By extension, I could hypothesize that the use of public space to make mobile phone calls violates our sensibilities in a variety of ways. One of them is the simple stimulation that occurs when others are in our presence. This simple physiological stimulation is also accompanied by some interesting collateral consequences, such as the fact that humans are likely to find themselves stimulated to perform better on tasks that they know well, but worse on those that are difficult or unfamiliar ("performance anxiety").

A further violation is that these others are engaged in acts of unreciprocated communication. As such, people are physiologically prepared to engage with them, yet they are engaged elsewhere. The problem of unreciprocated communication is one that seems highly problematical as it relates to mobile phone use. It has often been noted that people generally do not object to two people having a conversation in the seat behind us on a train. Yet people find it distracting when a person is talking on the mobile, that is, when there is not a conversational partner so that we can also hear the other half of the conversation.

Does Being a "Third Wheel" Make a Difference?

My research suggests that people do not mind mobile phone use of their partner when the "distant present" individual is a member of the in-group. This would account for the popularity of using mobiles at parties: the "distant other" can be included with the rest of "the gang." Problems, though, often arise when the "distant present" person is not seen as a member of the non-mobile phone-using partner. For instance, in focus groups many young people complain about their friends or paramours receiving calls from their buddies. These calls are ranked as highly irritating and can threaten an entire relationship (Rice and Katz, 2003).

It may very well be the case that if the distant other is unknown to the non-user ("third wheel"), the reactions that I have been discussion may continue to obtain. However, if the distant other is known, then it is quite likely that there will not be the negative reaction since the distant other will be seen as part of the in-group.

Specific Reactions in the Brain

Research has established that certain areas of the brain, and only those areas of the brain, are stimulated when humans see various facial expressions (Mark G. Frank, personal communication). This means that facial expressions have a phylogenetic component, and that they are about as hardwired as hardwiring can get. I do not know if there is a comparable process going on in terms of speech, though it may well be the case. The implications, though, are that people might have a difficult time not reacting to "half" of a conversation.

Liminal Transitions

The mobile phone is often used during transitions from place or activity. For example, I have commonly observed that the first thing people do in the U.S. upon exiting their car after having parked it is to check their phone for messages, or begin to make phone calls with it. Likewise, as people leave class buildings, they immediately begin using the mobile phone. Transitions—such as leaving a table after lunch with a friend or walking along the street—are also common locations for usage. They not only keep the individual company during these transitions, but also may provide a sense of reassurance. This is a topic that merits further investigation.

Ekistics

Let me return to the question of space, and touch on an important dimension in our examination of the question of the choreography of mobile communication in public places. Anthony Townsend has been a leader in examining the way in which mobile communication affects the use of urban space. Clearly, the field of ekistics— the science of human settlements, including urban or community planning and design—has much to offer in terms of integrating these devices into our social routines with the least harm (or even potential benefits added) to the quality of life. One observation that can be derived from the work in this field is that people generally find large, open urban spaces uncomfortable. They often feel anomic, isolated, frightened, or angst ridden. Having other human sharing that space, milling about, enjoying themselves, eliminates these feelings. This is true even if the other people in the shared open space are total strangers. Thus the mere presence of other active and engaged humans allays negative feelings that arise from being in a certain space. This is significant because when these strangers are on their mobile phones in these public spaces, they are no longer psychologically available. The sense of protection one might otherwise get from their presence is denied.

Moreover, studies have demonstrated that when drivers are using their mobile phones in the car, they are to a large degree mentally absent. These studies have been backed up by data about accidents and mobile phone usage. It would seem too that one is even visually absent to the mobile phone user on the street. Street talkers are so engrossed in their conversations that they do not apprehend what is going on around them despite their eyes being wide open. Hence, there may be substantial implications for the nature of urban public space due to the heavy usage of mobile phones. The evidence, as I read it, does not suggest that these reductions in the human qualities of public space are likely to be mere transient adjustments.

Historical Analogies Suggest Adjustment

My argument so far has heavily stressed the inflexible and "human nature" aspects of the way mobile phones are affecting our lives. There are obviously some arguments on the other side of the balance sheet. It may be that people will normalize. After a period of adjustment, we accept the presence of mobile phone conversations in public places without disturbance.

There are analogies that can be drawn from looking at issues and commentaries from a century ago by those who first experienced the telephone's potential for intrusiveness. For some of these involuntary technological pioneers, the recently introduced telephone was considered to be a heartless instrument of torture, ruining the lives of the sick and tired, opening homes to all varieties of evildoers (Marvin, 1988), and even a spreader of disease via unsanitary mouthpieces (Katz, 1999). Likewise, in the 1980s, a cottage industry of commentators was busy extolling the virtues of a clacking typewriter or even the scratching of quill pens in preference to the strange and inhuman process of using a computer to compose one's prose. (This line of discussion now seems quiescent).

The prospect of intercontinental air travel has gone from the status of a miracle to a humdrum burden. Moreover, no one needs reminding that there were, a century ago, so-called experts who thought that no human body could withstand the "extreme" experience of traveling at the speed of 100 km. per hour. Such footnotes to human history must make one cautious about asserting the limits of human behavior and capabilities of adjusting to change.

However, what the next phase of popular reaction will be remains unknown. Katie Cumiskey (2005) finds that Americans judge the "third wheel" to be isolated and unfortunate when examining mobile phone ads. I can also say that in informal surveys of Finnish users, who are among those who have had the longest exposure to the public use of mobile phones, substantial proportions say they are irritated by others' public use of the mobile phone. Certainly that was the conclusion of a national survey of the public's response to mobile phones conducted by Richard S. Ling who found that about 60 percent of the respondents said that public use of the mobile phone by others irritated them (University of Michigan, 2005).

Conclusion

Richard Sennett in his book, *The Fall of Public Man*, decried structural changes that have harmed the quality of modern urban life (Sennett, 1977). His list has been echoed in Robert Putnam's exhaustive *Bowling Alone* (Putnam, 2001). These concerns focus on diminished civic engagement, democratic mobilization, citizenship, quality social relationships, trust, and social capital.

Yet as important and valuable as these desiderata are, perhaps thought also should be devoted to understanding the subtle changes arising from widespread mobile phone usage. An important issue hangs over concerned citizens about questions such as what are we doing to our great public spaces. How are mobiles influential at the margins of social relationships and the moods and outlooks of those who are around the users? In addition, if it turns out that many of the effects of mobile phone usage are hardwired, as they may well be, how can experts design technology and build environments so as to moderate any negative effects?

The answer is not blowing in the wind nor is a weatherman needed to tell us, Bob Dylan's advice to the contrary notwithstanding. Rather the answer is within our grasp. It is the job of social scientists to get the needed information. Through high-quality research by communication scholars, analyses can be forthcoming that can help policymakers understand the stakes and assist the technologists in designing instruments and systems that meet many layers of individual and social needs. With insights gleaned from research on mobile phones, the intricate choreography of communication might become as pleasurable for the audience as it is for the performer.

Note

This chapter is based on A nation of ghosts? Choreography of mobile communication in public spaces. In K. Nyiri (Ed.), *Mobile Democracy: Essays on Society, Self and Politics*. Vienna: Passagen Verlag, 2004, pp. 21-32.

References

Clark, William R. and Michael Grunstei (2000). *Are we hardwired? The role of genes in human behavior*. New York: Oxford University Press.

Cumiskey, Kathleen M. (2005). Interpreting Public Mobile Phone Use: Studying its perceived impact on face-to-face interaction. Paper Presented at International Communications Association Pre-Conference Workshop on Mobile Communications. New York, New York.

Dawkins, Richard (1976). *The selfish gene*. New York: Oxford University Press.

Fortunati, Leopoldina (2002). Italy: stereotypes, true and false. In J. E. Katz and M.A. Aakhus (Eds.), *Perpetual contact: Mobile communication, private talk, public performance*. Cambridge: Cambridge University Press, pp. 42-62.

Fortunati, Leopoldina (2003). The mobile phone and democracy: An ambivalent relationship. In Kristof Nyiri (Ed.), *Mobile democracy: Essays on society, self and politics*. Vienna: Passagen Verlag, pp. 239-58.

Gould, Stephen Jay (1995). *Dinosaur in a haystack: Reflections in natural history*, New York: Crown.

Katz, James E. (1999). *Connections: Social and cultural studies of the telephone in American life*. New Brunswick, NJ: Transaction Publishers.

Katz, James E. and Mark Aakhus (Eds.) (2002). *Perpetual contact: Mobile communication, private talk, public performance*. Cambridge: Cambridge University Press.

Katz, James E. (Ed.) (2003). *Machines that become us: The social context of personal communication technologies*. New Brunswick, NJ: Transaction Publishers.

Ling, Richard S. (2004). *The Mobile connection: The cell phone's impact on society*. San Francisco, CA: Morgan Kauffman.

Marvin, Carolyn (1988). *When old technologies were new: Thinking about electric communication in the late Nineteenth Century*. New York: Oxford University Press.

Pinker, Steven (2002). *The blank slate: The modern denial of human nature*. New York: Viking.

Putnam, Robert (2001). *Bowling alone: The collapse and revival of American community*. New York: Simon and Schuster.

Rice, Ronald E. (1987). New patterns of social structure in an information society. In Jorge Schement and Leah Lieverouw (Eds.) *Competing visions, complex realities: Social aspects of the information society*. Norwood, NJ: Ablex, pp. 107-120.

Rice, Ronald E. (1999). Artifacts and paradoxes in new media. *New media and society*. 1 (1), 24-32.

Rice, Ronald E. and James E. Katz (2003). Mobile discourtesy: National survey results on episodes of convergent public and private spheres. In Kristof Nyiri (Ed.), *Mobile democracy: Essays on society, self and politics*. Vienna: Passagen Verlag, pp. 53-64.

Sennett, Richard (1977). *The fall of public man*. London: Faber and Faber.

Shell, Ellen Ruppel (2002). *The hungry gene: The science of fat and the future of thin*. New York: Atlantic Monthly Press.

Sugiyama, Satomi and James E. Katz (2003). Social conduct, social capital and the mobile phone in the U.S. and Japan: A preliminary exploration via student surveys. In Kristof Nyiri (Ed.), *Mobile democracy: Essays on society, self and politics*. Vienna: Passagen Verlag, pp. 375-385.

Tajfel, Henri and John Turner (1979). An integrative theory of intergroup conflict. In William G. Austin and Stephen Worchel (eds.), *The Social Psychology of Intergroup Relations*. Monterey, CA: Wadsworth, pp. 33-47.

University of Michigan (2005). Cell phone survey shows love-hate relationship. University of Michigan News Service, March 14. Retrieved from http://www.umich.edu/news/?Releases/2005/Mar05/r031405.

4

Public Performance of Mobile Telecommunication

Containing Mobile Communication: Early Ethos of Communication in Public

Using the telephone has always required some degree of performance on physical, oral and aural levels. Location too has been important in order to bring communication technology to the would-be communicator. The telephone booth originally conjoined access via convenience of location, containment of performance and privacy of usage. As a socio-technical artifact, the phone booth conjoined a sense of place for users to communicate to distant others, as well as degrees of separation from immediately co-located others. As part of the built environment, the changing design ethos of the phone booth reveals changes in standards of decorum and assumptions of lifestyle. Its evanescing from public space shows that current standards no longer require an individual to retreat from public view in order to have elaborate personal communication with distant others.

The telephone itself was a significant element early on amid considerations of the Modern. The power of instantaneous command, which the telephone conferred, often figured as a leitmotif of modernity. Early telephones reflected a preference for the fancy ornamentation of the Victorian and Edwardian eras—this fanciness was a leitmotif of the era, but also had an important social function, namely to disguise the proletarian principles of a machine (i.e., manual labor that should have been the province of the lower classes), and instead reflect a refined aesthetic standard for an el-

egant and tasteful home. This was as true for the telephones themselves as it was for their public presentation, namely in the form of
the public phone booth. Just as the telephone itself became stylized
and streamlined, so too did its public container, the phone booth
(See figures 4.1 and 4.2).

Figure 4.1
Illustration from First Patent for a Telephone Booth, Issued in 1883.
(Note wheels for mobility.)

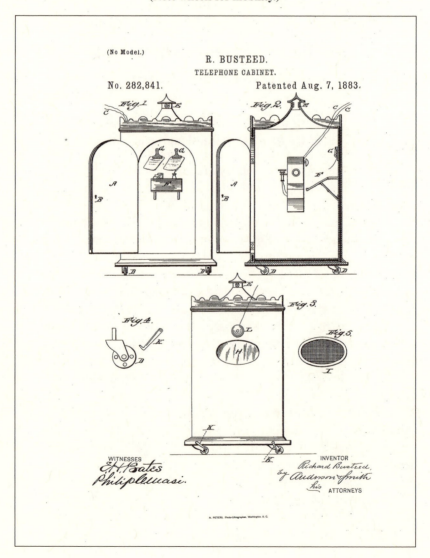

It is worthwhile taking a moment to inspect figure 4.1, which is the illustration accompanying the first U.S. patent for a telephone booth, issued in 1883. The design for a booth, or as it was then called, a cabinet, was granted a patent a mere seven years after the telephone itself had been invented by Alexander Graham Bell. The booth includes many features that might be considered modern, not only in terms of what technology could offer but also in terms of the needs of mobile phones users. Even though it was a cabinet, the design incorporated mobility as one of its features. It had wheels so, in the words of the inventor, "it may be moved from place to place when desired" (U.S. Patent Office, 1883). The cabinet also provided a messaging surface for taking notes, along with a pen, ventilation system, and a privacy screen. Another modern amenity and a feature important to today's mobile phones is that it also provided an alarm signal.

The 1883 telephone booth provides an interesting contrast to the later phone booths. In general, one can say that phone booths have had an evolution in form becoming ever smaller, sleeker, and more streamlined. The social presentation of phone booths has changed too. Ads for 1960s-era phone booth suggest a strong relationship between mobility, on the one hand, and communication and modernity, on the other. It even seems futuristic, as it indeed was. One early 1960s ad from the Bell System proclaims the "modern glass-and-aluminum booth...[is] a reassuring lighthouse along city streets and major highways. When you see it, you know service and protection are at hand.... Like the drive-in movie and the drive-in-bank, the Drive-Up Phone is a natural for a nation on wheels" (Bell System Telephone System Ad, ca. 1962, author's collection).

Technologies are also reflective of the specific social conditions and outlooks of each given historical era. The design of the phones followed the larger design impulse and adopted the "form follows function" shibboleth of the twentieth century. (The phrase has also been adopted by Nokia for their business line as "form meets function" as well as "styled for life," as proclaimed on its website promoting their 9300 model [Nokia, 2005].) Clearly, too, there has been an interplay and juxtaposition between different technologies of modernity and power, in this case the telephone and car. Both have symbolized the miracle of the machine age and freedom.

Figure 4.2
Bell Telephone System Advertisement for Telephone Communication Options for Mobile Users, ca. 1962.

THE AIRLIGHT BOOTH

Watson's woolly cave has grown into this modern glass-and-aluminum booth, used indoors or out. At night, it's a reassuring lighthouse along city streets and major highways. When you see it, you know that service and protection are at hand.

THE WALK-UP PHONE

As busy Americans make more and more calls, the Bell System makes service even more convenient. This newest public phone, called the Walk-Up, saves lots of time and steps. You'll find it as convenient as the corner mail box.

THE DRIVE-UP PHONE

Like the drive-in movie and drive-in bank, the Drive-Up Phone is a natural for a nation on wheels. Forget something? Late for a date? Need room reservations miles ahead? Just pull off the road and call — as you would on your own phone.

BELL TELEPHONE SYSTEM

There have been numerous attempts to deny the mobility of the mobile phone by creating mobile phone booths. One of the sleekest examples of this attempt is a mobile phone booth located in an SAS business-class lounge in Copenhagen's airport (figure 4.3). It is an attempt to handle the intrusive nature of the mobile phone, in a sense to make it immobile. There have been similar booths installed in U.S. airports by Verizon, which are also quite sleek (Metz, 2005). However, it does not appear that the technological prescription for managing manners and public space is becoming widely adopted. To the contrary, so far it is hardly being adopted at all.

Turning from the ways that have been devised to contain telephonic communication, the design aesthetics of the device itself needs to be addressed. Here the impulses of the modernist movement can be seen. In the next section, the broader setting within which the modernist enterprise has unfolded will be discussed and

Figure 4.3
Mobile Phone Booth in Copenhagen Airport Lounge

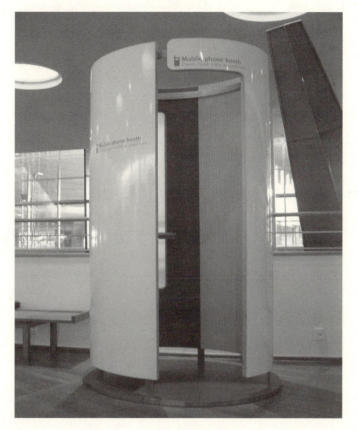

followed by an application of the modernist ethos to the marketing and consumption of the mobile phone.

Telephone as Aesthetic Expression

While powers of distant communication and control of tools of communication technology are status symbols, it is also the case that the telephone itself has developed within the context of the machine age. In particular, certain aesthetic ideas, such as modernism, have incorporated the telephone as part of its design thesis. In fact, the phone is often portrayed and understood as part of the future (advanced, streamlined) world. Modernism (see Everdell, 1997 for a review of modernism), which became increasingly powerful throughout the first two-thirds of the twentieth century, represents a sharp break with the adherence to traditional design motifs and modalities. That is, it wanted to replace tradition, which was most typically drawn from Classical and Medieval worlds. This old world would be replaced by a new one that emphasized spare stylization, streamlining, and a design ethos dictating that form should follow function, and nothing more.

An extreme form of modernism, known as Futurism, influenced many perceptions of the telephone and its meaning. As an ideological stance, Futurism emphasized speed, streamlining, and rapid motion. Excessively ornamental artifacts and handicraft products were to be dispensed with and, if possible, destroyed. Futurism's prime exponent was Filippo Tommaso Marinetti (1876-1944) who propounded his views in a 1909 manifesto, *Le Futurisme*. His credo included that "the world's magnificence has been enriched by a new beauty: the beauty of speed." Futurism and related movements reverberated quickly through elites of the industrialized world. Today, though superseded by other artistic movements they remain starkly visible and timely in mainstream design ethos and cultural speculations. They are also reflected in the design ethos of many telecommunication technologies.

It is worth recalling that the base of modernism and Futurism is rooted in the idea of the machine. This dialectic leads to tension between humans (with thoughts and feelings) and machines (perceived as having power and endurance). As one scholar has written, "Futurism was the first attempt in the Twentieth Century to re-invent life as it was being transfixed by new technologies and conceive of a new race in the form of machine-extended man" (Carey, 1993). There is indeed a long-standing theme in intellectual life of robots merging with humans (Katz, 2003) (a trend that appears a step closer to realization when one considers the headset-wearing mobile phone user increasingly prevalent on city streets).

There is another form of tension between public and private performance. Much of the trope of manners and the technologies that break or enforce them can be seen in the light of the tension between civilization and its discontents.

Nowadays, of course, the telephone has become mobile—it is taken out of our "back stage" areas of the home to the "front stage" of public life, where many onlookers can observe the self-presentation of others. The design of the mobile phone, led by the Modernist impulse, has become part of its possessor's fashion and personal expression. In the following sections, I will examine how the industry has been marketing this device as a modernistic item to the public, as well as how the public perceives it, focusing on the role of fashion and display.

Mobiles as Public Choreography

In an earlier volume entitled *Machines that Become Us: The Social Context of Personal Communication* (Katz, 2003), I discussed how the idea of the title, "machines becoming us" was applicable to the mobile phone. Among the reasons I gave was that the mobile phone could be our personal miniature representative. It was also used in the sense of "becoming" as in complementing and enhancing one's appearance. Fashion, Simmel (Simmel, 1957 [1904]) argued, encourages modification and adoption to individual needs. As Veblen (1934 [1899]) and others have pointed out, the wearing of fashionable attire enables individuals to separate themselves from their family, to develop a more distinct identity and a more unique sense of self, and yet maintain an affiliation with the prestigious aggregate (Fortunati, 1993; Lobet-Maris, 2003). Individuals can use fashion to tailor the social response they desire (Steele, 1997). Fashion, then, is a form of communication as well as an indicator of status and power. Taken together, these various senses of the word "becoming," can be thought of as links between technologies of communication and aesthetic traditions, which in turn are part of the cultural and hierarchy-producing processes.

Fortunati also argues the importance of "how to use" mobile phones in order to look "appropriate," and consequently, "fashionable." She states that knowing how to use the mobile with ease gives users prestige, and on the other hand, using it indiscreetly or anxiously and in continuous contact is considered vulgar (Fortunati, 2002). This suggests that mobile phone ownership in itself is not sufficient for evaluating the "fashionableness" of the mobile phone. The way people use the mobile phones is an important aspect that influences others' perception of "fashionableness."

Another aspect of mobile communication that would benefit from further investigation is the "urban environmental" effects of its use in public. To some degree, this has been investigated by Höflich (2004) and others. However, the physical performance of public communication, and its impact on the way others in the ambient environment behave, is not a well-developed area.

In this chapter, I would like to call attention to the value of further exploration of the way mobile phones are used in public. That is, greater attention could be profitably devoted to investigating mobile communication processes as part of the physical performances that individuals undertake as they share, navigate, and occupy public space. Perhaps it would be useful to apply the term "dance" to this process. In part, use of mobile communication in public is a dance form because the use of the mobile phone in public by one party often requires that the user's co-present partner adjust themselves in space and pace. That is, they must engage in a bit of choreography. This phenomenon of choreography finds a theoretical framework in Edward Hall's discussion of "being in sync" (Hall, 1977). Hall's idea notes that people in interactions need to "move together," and if one of the interactants is not "in sync," other parties find the interaction "disruptive" (Hall, 1977: p. 71). He further states:

> People in interactions move together in a kind of dance, but they are not aware of their synchronous movement and they do it without music or conscious orchestration. Being "in sync" is itself a form of communication. The body's message (in or out of awareness), whether read technically or not, seldom lie, and come much closer to what the person's true but sometimes unconscious feelings are than does the spoken word. (Hall, 1977: pp. 71-72).

Ling (2001) examines the way people manage their social interaction involving the mobile phone. Observations of mobile phone use in public places suggest that the emerging use of the mobile phone has introduced a new context wherein people need to move "in sync." Whether people are aware of their body movement or not, they adjust their body positioning once the face-to-face interactants start engaging in a mobile phone conversation, thus creating a kind of dance with the mobile phone. People involved in the interaction could be the partners of face-to-face conversation at the moment or people who happen to be physically present in public places, rather like the "forced eavesdropping" situation that Ling (2004) has described. The participants themselves could be mobile phone users, nonusers, or rejecters. Regardless of their mobile phone use, they all have to take into account the choreography of the mobile phone user to a degree, in order to have a smooth social interaction.

The choreography of arrangement is informal, but seems remarkably consistent within cultures. For instance, it has been argued that in Japan, users in public conveyances emphasize manners and privacy, seeking to exclude others. What follows are summaries of our observation. First, the non-using partner has to engage in symbolic behaviors that suggest valuable activity. At the same time, there is lots of tacit and audible but indirect coordination. For instance, as the mobile phone user gets ready to conclude the conversation, the non-participating partner mysteriously is able to resume focus on the mobile phone user, and begin engaging the user visually.

In addition, behavior tends to reproduce itself. In his discussion of "postural echo," Desmond Morris observes that friends who are informally speaking with one another often adopt similar body postures. They do this, he says, "unconsciously as part of a natural body display of companionship" (Morris, 1977: p. 83). I would go further, and suggest that it is often the case that people adopt the postures and body positions of those around them whether or not they are friends.

While Morris holds that this form of imitation is not deliberate, I would again go further and argue that it is actually quite hard to resist. It can often only be done if one is consciously making an effort not to do so. At the very least, there is a continual process of body posture interaction that complements the postures of those around the actor.

In the case of mobile phone use, the co-present partner, who had not been using his/her mobile phone, will often be prompted to begin using his/her own phone. Certainly our surveys of students in classrooms reinforce this idea. Students often say that when they see another student using a mobile, it prompts them to begin doing so even if they had not originally been intending to do so. Mobile phone use in public therefore seems to beget still more public mobile phone use.

Mobiles and Co-Present Posture Partners

Consider the situation of two people "'walking t;gether in public, which from a proxemics perspective creates a *pas de deux*. However, assume additionally that one of the people has a mobile phone; this can change "postural echoes" considerably. They may no longer signify "companionship" but rather reflect the demands of relationship juggling. In such cases, the mobile phone user may be trying to send relational messages alternately to both the co-present and the distant companion. Concomitantly, the non-mobile phone using person may still seek to display companionship, and thus unconsciously echo the behavior of the partner who is physically present and using the mobile phone.

When one member of a dyad is on the mobile and the other not, an intermittent checking of the phone partner's expression takes place, often when the partner is looking away. This is be followed by the "looking" person looking away, and then "phoning" partner then checking out the non-phoner's face. A seeming ping-pong game of glances ensues.

Looks and body language alone are not the complete picture of the mobile phone dance. There is "song" too. The tone and loudness of the phone person's voice signals the partner as to what the partner should expect in terms of distance and anticipated additional time on that the phone users will be on talking; this too helps coordinate the choreography of the dyad or, more properly, triad.

Multitasking in Public

Still another area not well understood is the question of multitasking, of what happens when mobile phone users try to do several things at once. Multitasking is posing some interesting challenges to businesses as well providing entertainment and humor for public observers. Some establishments have tried to use signage or announcements to prevent mobile phone users from multitasking while conducting their business in public. For instance, at the storied Lincoln Center in New York City signs are posted near ticket booths forbidding patrons from using their cell phone while on queue. Nonetheless, despite social and institutional disapproval, mobile technology users are becoming more adept at using their devices while performing other activities. Some of the negative consequences of increased multitasking were discussed in chapter 3. Still, it is clear that users will continue to expand their repertoires to be able to use their mobile communication devices while engaged in other activities, thereby modifying public choreography.

A corollary aspect of public phone performance is that sometimes the dynamic of mobile phone use is largely (or even exclusively) for those who are present. That is, talking on (or playing with) the mobile phone may be as much for the benefit of those "present" with a mobile phone user as it is of those who are "absent" and would be the putative subjects of the mobile phone use. (This is certainly confirmed by small-scale research I have undertaken with students that shows about one in four mobile phone users say they have pretended to talk on the mobile phone when there was actually no one on the other end of the line. See chapter 1).

So the choreography of mobile communication performance needs to be better understood as an interpersonal communication phenomenon, as a physical as well as a psycho-social and organizational phenomenon.

But can public performance of mobile communication usage truly qualify as a form of folk dance? I believe it does. Part of the reason is due to the public performance and ritualistic nature of the amateur performers, as sketched above. Yet it is also due to the changing understanding of what dance is, especially from the vantage point of professional dance companies and choreographers as well as academics. Increasingly, contemporary theatrical dance companies are exploring quotidian elements. Growing numbers of choreographers are devoting themselves to a *Nouvelle* dance approach that draws from the lived experience on the street and in daily life. These efforts attempt to break through the conceits of formal approaches of dance and present raw and "undisciplined" performances. Artificial costumes are dispensed with in favor of ordinary street clothes (Vaccarino, 2003). The choreography of Merce Cunningham and Gilbert and George provide examples. Both sets of artists seem to offer "high art" reflections and refractions of what millions engage in on a daily basis. What musician John Cage said of Merce Cunningham may be equally germane to the public performance of mobile phone users and the soundscape they create. Cage argues that Cunningham's choreography dispenses with linear elements of either a narrative or psychological nature. Neither, in the words of John Cage, "does it rely on a movement towards and away from climax. As in abstract painting, it is assumed that an element (a movement, a sound, a change of light) is in and of itself expressive; what it communicates is in large part determined by the observer himself" (Cunningham, undated.). So it is with the choreography of mobile phone performance; it can be readily understood, and studied, equally as an interpersonal communication phenomenon or as a rhythmic interpretation of a folk dance. This also is an area that deserves additional scholarly analysis in the coming years.

Body Display of Equipment

In order to use the mobile phone as an enhancement of self-image, how the mobile phone is carried and displayed becomes an issue. As a result, new opportunities are created in terms of fashion and display to carry and put mobile phones into operation. These include phone devices that flash brightly when in use to signal to ambient others that the device owner is important and/or connected enough to be talking to a distant person.

The dependence and ease of use exigencies concerning the mobile phone encourage creative solutions. Clothes and backpacks have been designed to integrate conveniently the mobile phone into what is worn. Digithongs (www.digithongs.com) offers around-the-body carrier straps and describes itself as an "innovative line of cellular phone accessories created to meet the needs of women." Another firm, Dockers, makes the "Mobile Pant" (Newman and Wendland, 2002). In 2005, I spotted pants for hip teens and pre-teens being sold; they had bright signs stapled to two of the several pockets stating they were for cell phones; most school backpacks also seem to be designed with a cell phone pocket.

As users load themselves down with more gadgets, specialized harnesses have been created. More substantial than a thong is the "Scott eVest," which is designed to hold electronic equipment in numerous zip, flap and Velcro pockets. It even has additional pockets inside some of the pockets. For headphone wires there are hidden tunnels within the clothing. Another example of tech fashion cladding that seems to combine geek and chic is the e-harness, which is similar to the undercover agent's twin armpit holsters. Although these harnesses are not common, they are occasionally seen on "road warriors" in the New York metropolitan area.

Despite the plentitude of clothing enhancements and accessories, many users rely on their own creativity rather than commercial products to park their phones. Indeed, as the mobile phone becomes more commonplace, users are finding ever more convenient places on the body to park their mobile devices, sometimes with comic or flirtatious effect.

Artistic Recreation

Other researchers have discussed how people behave relative to their bodies and their mobiles (Fortunati, 1993; 2003; Kaiser, 2003; de Gournay, 2002). But my goal here is to have added a more precise connection between industrial ethos of marketing a futuristic status symbol and the folk artistic aesthetic re-incorporation of an important and socially significant device. Public performance dimensions have been underscored. As to the folk dimension, the aim has been to show this in terms of artistic endeavors reflected in mobile phone use, consumption, and multitasking.

The analysis presented in this chapter is at variance with theories of mass society, and of cultural studies of oppression, both of which suggest the consumer is a passive cow, milked by large corporations. Here another image is presented, which of course does not necessarily rule out the plausibility of these other intellectual traditions. That is, the perspective offered here suggests that consumers find an exquisite technology which fits extremely well with their values and interests, and that they adopt it in droves. Nevertheless, users are more than mere consumers. They are also co-creators. They demonstrate this by further manipulating these devices after purchase to reflect personal tastes and to represent themselves to the outside world. The mobile phone then may be seen as a "necessary accessory" to the body, as Leopoldina Fortunati (Fortunati, 2002: p. 58) has pointed out. It becomes not simply a communication device but a reflection and embodiment of the user.

In doing so, users are engaging in the same impulse that led to cosmetics and jewelry at the dawn of civilization. It is the same impulse that leads people to decorate their homes, apartments and gardens. Profound and ancient aesthetics are being incorporated into the seemingly thoroughly modern mobile phone.

Note

This chapter is based on, Il corpo fra creatività artistica e tecnologica, with Satomi Sugiyama. Workshop presentation, MART conference, Rovereto, Italy, November 8, 2003.

References

Birdwhistell, Ray L. (1964). *Introduction to kinesics*. Ann Arbor, MI: University Micro-films.

Cunningham, Merce (Undated). Merce Cunningham. Retrieved from http://www.merce.org/merce_bio.html.

de Gournay, Chantal (2002). Pretence of intimacy in France. In J. E. Katz and M. Aakhus (Eds.), Perpetual contact: Mobile communication, private talk, public performance. Cambridge: Cambridge University Press, pp. 193-205.

Fortunati, Leopoldina (1993). *Gli italiani al telefono*. Milan: Franco Angeli.

Fortunati, Leopoldina (2002). Italy: stereotypes, true and false. In J. E. Katz and M.A. Aakhus (Eds.), *Perpetual Contact: Mobile Communication, Private Talk, Public Performance*. Cambridge: Cambridge University Press, pp. 42-62.

Höflich, Joachim (2004). Part of two frames: Mobile communication and the situational arrangement of communicative behavior. Conference, Budapest, April 24-25. Mobile Communication: Social and Political Effects.

Kaiser, Susan B. (2003). Fashion, media, and cultural anxiety. Visual representations of childhood. In Fortunati, Leopoldina, James E. Katz and Raimondá Riccini (Eds.) (2003). *Mediating the human body, Technology, communication, and fashion*. Mahwah, NJ: Lawrence Erlbaum Associates, pp. 155-161.

Ling, Richard (2001). The social juxtaposition of mobile telephone conversations and public spaces. *Telenor R&D Report*, 45/2001.

Metz, Rachel (2005). Booths silence cell-phone boors. Wired News, September 02. Retrieved from http://www.wired.com/news/culture 0,1284,68997,00.html?tw=wn_tophead_5

Nokia (2005). Nokia: Connecting people. Retrieved from http://www.nokiaforbusiness.com/amer/9300/

U.S. Patent Office (1883 [2005]). Telephone-cabinet, patent 282,841, issued August 07, 1883.

Vaccarino, Elisa (2003). Corpo danzante, corpo mutante. Paper presented at "Il corpo fra creatività artistica e tecnologica," MART conference, Rovereto, Italy, November 7- 8.

5

Mobile Phones as Fashion Statements: The Co-Creation of Mobile Communication's Public Meaning

This chapter explores public mobile communication technology as a design aesthetic. It addresses the mobile phone from the standpoint of its commercial origins and public consumption. The discussion emphasizes fashion and identity in the co-creation and consumption of mobile communication technology. The mobile phone is analyzed as both a physical icon and as an item of decorative display related to fashion and design and popular culture.

I begin by noting how the early telephone, because it enabled people to communicate efficiently over distance, served as a status symbol. I then highlight the role of fashion and display to show how the symbolic meaning of telecommunication has been evolving. In terms of fashion, I look at the way fashion and styles have been used to promote the mobile phone by industry. In terms of display, I look at the collateral promotion of other products by reference to the mobile phone and body-technology relationship. Finally, I examine co-constructions that extend beyond the narrow, utilitarian purposes for which the mobile phone was originally designed to show how novel links are forged to deeper psychological and existential processes. That is, the mobile phone is strongly connected with ingrained human perceptions of distance, power, status, and identity.

A few words concerning formal theory may be in order. Among the most prominent and influential sub-perspectives of the functionalist school are the "domestication" and "uses and gratifications" perspectives. They have been frequently employed by earlier researchers on mobile communication (e.g., Haddon, 2003; Leung and Wei, 1999; Leung and Wei, 2000; Wei and Lo, 2003). They continue to exert substantial influence despite some criticism of their logical clarity. In this chapter, by contrast, the expressive and symbolic dimensions of technology are emphasized. These dimensions seem critical in understanding the reception and use of mobile communication technology. Indeed, in some cases they may actually supersede utilitarian motives in their importance. Certainly this view has been argued by Fortunati and her associates generally (Fortunati, Katz and Riccini, 2003) and more narrowly in what has been dubbed the Apparatgeist theoretical perspective (Katz and Aakhus, 2002). From the expressive perspective, as argued in previous chapters, many mobile phone users are engaging in the same impulse that led to cosmetics and jewelry at civilization's dawn. The mobile phone thus becomes a device that is not merely a tool but a miniature aesthetic statement about its owner as well. In a word, fashion. Fashion is an important form of symbolic communication that can drive human behavior. Therefore, as an aid to understanding the way people use the mobile phone, it is meaningful to consider the relationship between fashion and the mobile phone.

Fashion and the Mobile Phone

Davis (1985) discusses ambivalent feelings that people experience about fashion. According to him, aambivalence in fashion includes "the subjective tension of youth versus age, masculinity versus femininity, androgyny versus singularity, inclusiveness versus exclusiveness, work versus play, domesticity versus worldliness, revelation versus concealment, license versus restraint, and conformity versus rebellion" (Davis, 1985: p. 24-25). These binary tensions are likely to occur when people situate their "self" in certain social groups. Kaiser (1998) notes that the identity ambivalence is especially evident in many cultures today where society and fashion rapidly change. This, in turn, suggests that the ambivalence related to fashion comes from people's emotional need to keep abreast of fashion changes in order to maintain their social identity. And this ambivalence fosters people's attentiveness toward fashion changes. It is within this fast-changing fashion environment in the modern world, that technologies have been adopted as accessories in our presentation of self, and thus, incorporated into repertoire of "personal front" (Goffman, 1959). The way people select the designs and brand of wristwatches is a good example of this, and such a phenomenon seems to have extended to the way people select the mobile phone.

There is increasing attention to fashion and technology as an outgrowth of a growing interest in the sociology of the body. Among the topics is how technology is incorporated into clothing and displayed on the body (Fortunati, 2002). Fortunati considered social implications of mobile phone use in Italy, focusing on its aesthetic dimension. She attributes the success of the mobile phone in Italy to its "fashionableness." Consequently, she argues, it has become a "necessary accessory" (p. 54). She also points out that the mobile was associated with the higher classes in Italian society until quite recently. Thus, according to Fortunati, "the mobile is an accessory that enriches those who wear it, because it shows just how much they are the object of communicative interest, and are thereby desired, on the part of others" (p. 54). Fortunati's argument suggests an interesting point that mobile phone ownership and its use communicate "about" the person. This leads us to think about the mobile phone not just as a tool to "talk" but also as a means to communicate symbolically about the self. The mobile phone influences how people perceive others as well as whether people would hope to have a personal relationship, and it in turn influences how people decide to incorporate the mobile phone into their self-images.

Communication over distance is a status marker, as noted at several junctures in this volume. Until quite recently, communication over great distance was in all societies extraordinarily expensive if not downright impossible. Only supernatural beings or an occasional shaman were considered capable of such feats. Greek mythology did not even attribute this power to most of its pantheon. Against this backdrop, it is little wonder that those with access to modern communication innovations become imbued with status. This was true of the early telephone itself when it was first deployed more than one hundred years ago (Marvin, 1988). It is also true for the early era of the mobile phone.

From another perspective, though, early adopters were of interest since they were also the cutting edge showing the rest of society what was likely to become an everyday technology. As is true for many other technologies, such as air conditioning, automobiles, and computers, early adopters were in a sense living in the near future—they were already experiencing, to a greater or lesser extent, what life would be like for subsequent adopters. Early adopters were by their experiences and behavior also helping shape and drive the future. The way they chose to use the technology and how they reconfigured their own interactional repertoires in light of their experiences was also creating (and sometimes foreclosing) norms and practices that would be available eventually to the bulk of subsequent users.

Futuristic and Modern: Industry's Presentation of the Mobile Phone to the Public

Much of the public presentation of the mobile phone has been carefully crafted. This, obviously, is also typical of other commercialized products (Himmelstein, 1993). An aim of this chapter is to deepen understanding of the themes that have been highlighted in the design of the mobile phone and in mobile phone ad campaigns.

When a usable mobile phone burst upon the scene in the late 1980s, it appeared to the public as a highly futuristic and sophisticated technology. It was an emblem of the rich and important, though not yet the famous. Interestingly, a document published by Motorola indicates that its early StarTac clamshell mobile phone was inspired by the communicator of the TV series, *Star Trek* (Motorola, 2003); certainly the name chosen for the line, "StarTac" reinforces this belief (Bormanis, undated).

In terms of handsets themselves, manufacturers from the outset may have wanted to have an explicit futuristic and high-status design look for the mobile telephone. Although this cannot be demonstrated directly because the archives of the design processes of mobile phone manufacturers remain proprietary, certainly there is scattered evidence to support this view. For instance, there have been various public discussions by leaders of design teams. Thus, Alastair Curtis, director of a Nokia design group, has said, "Design has been one of the key elements in the products from Day 1" (Swartz, 2003). Frank Nuovo, Nokia's chief designer, indicated that his design ethos is based on elegant simplicity, relying on high-end accessories for inspiration (Hafner, 1999). Of a specific handset device—Motorola's StarTac, the wildly popular clamshell design of the 1990s—a Motorola designer said, "We wanted a phone that would be visible enough to express something about you. . . . It started as a couture product" (Oehmke, 1999).

A modern, futuristic design impulse has been strongly articulated in the advertising campaigns for mobile communication, according to several scholarly studies of mobile phone ads. For instance, based on semiotic analysis, Pajnik and Lesjak-Tušek (2002) suggest that the image of what they define interchangeably as "Modernity" and "Western values" are important themes in mobile phone ads deployed in Slovenia. In another study on China, conducted by Zhang and Harwood (2004), it appears that household appliances, including telephones and computers, are often associated with "modernity" in advertising themes. According to Zhang and Harwood, although the TV advertising of these new technologies also employs traditional cultural values (e.g., family [and societal identity]) in conjunction with the "modern" theme, it is noteworthy that "modernity" was one of the most frequently used value themes in recent Chinese TV advertising. In an analysis of the famous "1984" Macintosh advertisement, Stein (2002) argues that the ad employed the "freedom" and "revolution" rhetoric, which set a tone for later advertising for other new technologies such as Microsoft Windows and mobile phones.

These studies underscore the fact that the mobile is presented to the public via advertisements as an embodiment of youth, modernism, and futurism. Researchers find a consistent presence of "modern," "cutting-edge," and "futuristic" themes in the way sophisticated consumer technologies are represented to various national cultures. Were these themes lacking in appeal to consumers, it is implausible that marketers would continue to spend lavishly on them. In other words, modernity resonates in the minds of the consumer and therefore sells. What continues to be sold is what is continued to be designed. Contrarily, despite ad blitzes, if something does not catch on with the public, it disappears. (This situation is exemplified by aggressively merchandized products which despite being highly promoted have failed. Examples include "'New' Coca-Cola," Apple's hand-held device called Newton, and a thick beverage aimed as a meal substitute called "Metrical.") A significant part of the argument is that the ads do not consistently trick or force people into thinking they want something so much as they capitalize upon latent desires or suggest new ones. However, the motive has to appeal to the consumer and serve the consumer's interest. This line of reasoning is contrary to those who say that such ads are hegemonic moves by media/advertising industries to foster consumerism and certain social values. People seem to like these themes on their own.

Nonetheless, the industry has also sought to be sure that the public would apprehend the technology as being of high status and socially desirable. Nokia provides a good example of this process as it participates in the production of numerous Hollywood films and programs. Its futuristic image was intentionally supplemented with one of status. Thus, as part of a product placement scheme, Nokia phones appeared on popular TV shows (*Beverly Hills 90210; Friends*) and were distributed gratis to Hollywood stars in an effort to build cachet (Oehmke,1999). Nokia paid handsomely to have a special model shown off in a James Bond film, as well as in the first *Matrix* film (which featured the Nokia 8110). Additionally, Nokia has paid for product placements in the films *Charlie's Angels*, and *Minority Report* as well as TV shows such as *The X-Files* and *The Sopranos* (Snellman, 2003). Said a Nokia marketing vice president, "If Tom Cruise transmits crucial evidence with his Nokia phone, many viewers may realize they need a camera phone too" (Snellman, 2003).

Nokia is not the only mobile phone manufacturer who is aware of the importance of influencing public images of the mobile phone. Observing Nokia's success, Sony Ericsson was able to displace Nokia in a subsequent Bond film, *Die Another Day*, while Samsung was the mobile phone star in the sequel *Matrix Reloaded*. For one cycle of the Emmy's, Nokia sent their newest mobile phone to all the Emmy award winners. These efforts have paid off in brand status and recognition. Interbrand, a consulting firm, says its research shows that Nokia is the eleventh most recognized brand, and that it even ranks ahead of Mercedes-Benz. Said one Interbrand official: Nokia is "selling an image, not technology.... They're very good at technology, but image is the key" (Hafner, 1999).

So, up to this point, the argument is that the mobile phone has been presented to the public as a modern and image-enhancing technology. It is not only presented as modern and cutting-edge, however. In the next section, the way the mobile phone has also been marketed as a high-fashion item is discussed.

Fashion Imaging in Contemporary Mobile Phone Ads

The cultural construct of jewelry and fashion is heavily laden with gender-specific connotations; but so too is the social construction of the telephone, as Claude Fischer, Lana Rakow, and more recently Kalpana David have demonstrated (Fischer, 1992; Rakow, 1992; David, 2004). The active but feminine and always youthful woman is often an iconic image used in the promotion of mobile phones.

The emphasis on stylish design, elite status, and fashion appears to have been a central part of marketing. There is no sign of the trend abating in terms of marketing mobiles as exclusive fashion and trend-setting style items. A July 1, 2004 press release from Motorola claims that "New York City Elite Flip over the New Motorola A630." The release bubbles on: "Staged on the rooftop of New York City's exclusive Hotel, top celebrities and style leaders were among the first to witness the unveiling of the next 'must have' mobile device from Motorola" (Motorola, 2004).

Gender and Body Relationships in the Promotion of Mobile Phones

While it is not my intention to survey the entire field of ads for mobile phones, it would be useful to look at some particular ads, especially those that have been prominently placed. Obviously, the ads I mention are not necessarily statistically representative of all ads, nor am I including business-oriented ads. However, it is nonetheless worthwhile to look at particular and concrete instances of the way the mobile phone has been promoted to the public. In particular, I will examine some body and gender relationships depicted in ads appearing in 2004 and 2005. These are chosen as illustrations, not as proof and not necessarily as a representative sample of ads one presumably encounters.

In Budapest's airport, in spring 2004, a large, backlit billboard-style ad depicts two high-fashion items: a luxury watch and a designer purse. These fashion items are accompanied by a Siemens phone. The equivalence is clear: a Siemens phone is a fashion item.

Other images that emphasize the fashion display of the mobile phone are ads for Motorola's Moto line. One ad in my collection appeared in a magazine for young women published in the U.S. The ad depicts a mobile phone handset displayed literally as a piece of body jewelry. In this case the mobile phone seems to be a form of navel-jewelry, inserted in the navel as a result of piercing. It would certainly seem that the advertiser (in this case Motorola) is seeking to give its product an edgy and ultra-hip image consonant with current fashion. One appeal of body piercing is as a form of risk and youthful status, and in this case the advertisers appear to be trying to associate these values with mobile phone use. Certainly the idea of piercing the abdomen of a young female is rich with symbolic sexual and sadomasochistic connotations.

The larger visual environment can be substantially saturated by mobile phone ads. This seems particularly true in terms of airports, as suggested previously. But the lateral space of an airport can provide a unique environment within which to promote mobile phones. For instance, the long corridors can be used to project extended images of mobile phones as statements of fashion and lifestyle. One such depiction occurred in July 2004 at the Schiphol (Netherlands) airport. The ad was perhaps fifty meters long and two meters high. It contained photos of a group of girls on a beach sun bathing, handing a mobile phone to one another. They would seem to be active, hip, daring, and hedonistic. The linking of their phones and bodies emphasizes the social and clique nature of a mobile-leisure lifestyle. The close collocation of the bodies suggests far greater intimacy than is generally observed in Western Europe and North America (Goffman 1974; 1979).

Figure 5-1
Group of Sunbathing Girls in a Vodaphone Ad Displayed at Schiphol (Amsterdam) Airport

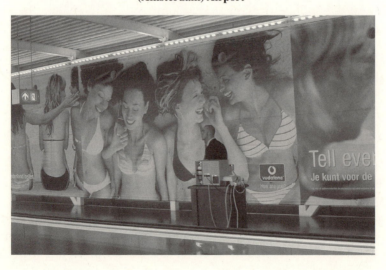

In my non-systematic collecting activity, I have also encountered numerous ads made by mobile phone companies depicting a woman grasping a man from behind while talking to a distant other on the mobile. In many cases, the female in these ads appears to be "riding" the male, and her arm covers his breast. It does not take a great deal of imagination to see imagery of domination and close physical relationships being depicted in these ads.

While by no means definitive evidence, nonetheless taken together these images provides reasonable grounds to believe that fashion and body display are important aspects in the depictions used by advertisers to sell mobile phones. Many of the depictions are of active women and girls, often dominating or controlling men

Figure 5.2
Female Riding on Male in a Mobile Phone Ad Displayed in Schiphol
(Amsterdam) Airport

(or men are absent altogether). To the extent these images exist in mobile phone ads, it suggests that those feminist perspectives that say commercialism is designed to humiliate, diminish, or control women relative to men are in need of revision. The next topic is the reception of the mobile phone by consumers, highlighting the perceptions of users and the way they modify the technology to serve as identity objects.

Consumer Perception and Reception

How does the public perceive mobile communication technology? There is evidence that some parts of the public evaluate it in terms of fashion and status, that is, in the same way that the mobile phone industry also seeks to project it to the public. (The reader is reminded that it is the case that there is a reciprocal process of negotiating meanings between an industry seeking to frame the technology and the public that responds to, adopts, and modifies further the technology.) The importance of fashion in the consumer mind is suggested by a variety of findings from our focus group interviews and surveys.

In 2001, Satomi Sugiyama (Katz and Sugiyama, forthcoming) conducted a focus group interview with college students at a U.S. university. Most of the participants at first said that they did not think of the mobile phone as a fashion item. However, a college student from Korea said, "For our culture, [the] cell phone is a part of the fashion thing. Yes, especially for [the] younger generation, it kind of tells your personality, and it tells many things." Interestingly, this statement prompted other participants to reconsider their original response, and they started talking about how young people use the mobile phone for fashion. A female participant said, "for [the] younger generation, they don't need [the] cell phone, because they are not in college. High school, middle school...because I see younger kids having cell phones. I think they think it fashion [able]." And another participant followed by saying It's changing. People are switching their phones...I don't' know, I think some people are trying to be cool about it.

Sugiyama observed some ambivalence about how to understand the mobile phone and fashion in this focus group. Participants sense some association between the growingly ubiquitous mobile phone around them and fashion, but the association did not seem to be very clear in their minds. There seemed to be a kind of "third-person effect" operating, so that while they see themselves using the mobile phone for necessity they see others as having a style dimension to their evaluations. This suggests that the mobile phone, in young people's discourse, takes on the role of a fashion accessory that is in great demand as a status symbol. A national survey taken in 2004 of youngsters in the U.S. concluded that for eight- to ten-year-olds the mobile phone is "as much a status symbol as a communications device" (Selingo, 2004).

In 2002, Satomi Sugiyama and I investigated the relationship between the timing of the mobile phone adoption and the importance of the aesthetic dimension of the phone (Katz and Sugiyama, forthcoming). The results indicated that American youths who adopted mobile phones earlier were more likely to think that the style of the mobile phone would be an important factor in selecting their own mobile phone. A similar trend was found in the sample group of Japanese youths (Katz and Sugiyama, forthcoming). In addition, our research showed that both U.S. and Japanese heavy mobile phone users valued style more relative to non-light users. Moreover, Japanese heavy users even preferred style over battery life. If one considers the battery life of the mobile phone as a functional aspect and style as an aesthetic aspect, our research seems to suggest that many buyers, especially early adopters and heavy users among youth, trade off functionality willingly for attractive styling. (Of course, the mobile phone is not unique in this regard, since many people choose aesthetic or fashion appeal over functionality in many areas, including in their choice of shoes, and even of political candidate. But the point is that there is an affective as well as instrumental motive at work here.)

In a 2004 poll of our own, we surveyed a class of Rutgers undergraduate students about their attitudes towards mobile communication and fashion. The class was for non-technologists on the subject of information and technology and most students were about twenty years old; fortuitously, exactly 100 students (out of about 114 students attending that day) completed the survey, so percentages and number of respondents align exactly. Like the above surveys, the poll is not representative of all Rutgers students. Nevertheless, it may shed some light on the relative frequency and intensity of attitudes towards mobile phone fashion. Over half the students agreed with the statement that "my mobile phone should look cool" and of those about half (i.e., twenty-five) also indicated that they notice the fashionableness of the mobile phones of their friends. (The category of "agree" and "strongly agree" were collapsed for the purposes of this analysis.) In other words, about a quarter of the students surveyed appear to be actively engaged in a fashion assessment of mobile phones. This would seem to be a striking figure, although it bears repeating that this is not a representative sample and cannot tell us to what extent, if any, the campaigns of the mobile phone industry influence the perception and attitudes of the students. Nonetheless, it is noteworthy that there is a similarity between the way the industry has been promoting the mobile phone and the way young users perceive it. At the other end of the spectrum, however, we must mention that ten students disagreed with the statements, apparently rejecting interest in the fashionableness of the mobile phones of both themselves and their friends. Of course, we never meant to suggest that all users view the mobile phone as a fashion or status symbols, which they clearly do not. Rather it is the case that many do, and that this perception is important for commercial success of companies as well as the use of public space and the condition of individual lives. We turn our attention to this topic next.

Buyers of mobile phones may be clustered into two broad categories. First are those who purchase one simply as a communication tool, claiming to care little about its appearance or symbolism. Though immensely important to the overall market, this cluster is not the focus of this chapter. Second are those who buy one in part because of the status that a design, logo, or brand imparts. They are the group to which the preceding discussion concerning style is addressed. Many mobile phones adopters seek to individualize, personalize, and integrate them into their own local cultural meaning. Within this second approach, the concept of having the device be a symbol of individuality is important. "Our primary concern is to tailor products as much to the individual as possible," according to Alastair Curtis, director of Nokia's design group. "The phone is an extension of your identity" (Swartz 2003). People respond, often making a conscious choice of the style of their mobile phone (Ling, 2003; Oksman and Rautiainen, 2003). This process has been investigated in other domains in terms of consumerism and identity (Massaris, 1997). In exactly the same way that people employ "fashion" to express their identity (e.g., Davis, 1992; Crane, 2000), they consume the mobile phone.

In order to underscore the element of prestige in a technology that is becoming omni-present, there has been a figurative arms race towards ever more lavish mobile phones. One approach, from the London-based boutique company, Vertu, has been the marketing of especially made high-end phones, which are also a form of expensive jewelry. This fashion item has platinum casing and a sapphire crystal screen. (It is also designed so that the phone's internal technology can be easily updated.) The price is about $26,000. It is worth noting in this context that Vertu was formed by Nokia in 2002, clearly as a part of its fashion-luxury initiative. Motorola recently launched a clamshell V600 model that offers interchangeable covers studded with clear Swarovski crystals, and offers a variety of fashion handbags in which to carry its phones. Nokia's recently introduced 7200 model offers fabric covers that have analysts calling it the Louis Vuitton phone. While the emphasis on luxury is not a guarantee of success, it nonetheless shows that at least the handset manufacturers are persuaded that such an approach will appeal to an important market segment.

The phenomenon of transforming the mobile phone into high-fashion jewelry is observable in other parts of the world as well. Gem-encrusted handsets have become extremely popular in China, which is experiencing rapid growth of mobile phone use. In 2000, TCL Mobile began offering diamond-studded mobile phones. TCL Mobile sold more than 12 million jeweled phones between 2001 and mid-2003 (most of which had fake gems) (Reuters, 2004).

"In Asia, phones are much more of an aspirational statement about who you are and who you want to be," Scott Durchslag, a Motorola corporate vice president said. TCL Mobile's managing director, Wan Ming Jian, asserts that in Asia, "attaching jewelry on the phone adds a cultural and spiritual dimension to the product." In further describing the popularity of jeweled phones, Mr. Wan said that "to many Chinese, precious stones symbolize esteem, good fortune, peace and love. So jeweled mobile phones are not just communication tools, they also act as lucky charms" (Reuters, 2004). This reinforces the importance of the cultural setting in considering the meaning of the mobile phone.

Although certain styles of the mobile phone are associated with high fashion and prestigious brands, of course anything done by style leaders is subject to cooptation by the hoi polloi, thus diluting the brand's status value (which is always a challenge to fashion as

Veblen noted). Nowadays it is common in department stores to see jewelry for adorning a mobile phone. (Notably, these items are offered not in the electronics section but in the jewelry section.) Street fairs too are a venue for mobile phone enhancements. As popular as these items are in the U.S., they are even more so in Korea and other Asian countries.

Clearly, a growing segment of the public purchases these ready-made, futuristic-looking devices but then personalizes them. That is, they alter the appearance of the device to make it more individually meaningful and symbolic within their cultural contexts. Pasted-on photos, colored plates, dangling antenna ornaments, and fake jewels are common "after-market" enhancements added by users. "With the colors, symbols, patterns and brands people choose, they are associating themselves with the meaning conveyed by them," according to Chris Conley, design professor at Illinois Institute of Technology (Swett, 2002) (see chapter 4). Again, it is worthwhile reminding the reader that the mobile phone is not unique in this regard, since other consumer items are also enhanced and customized by users, including bicycles, jeans, and backpacks. Still the extent and meaningfulness of personalization, as well as the substantial outlays of money and time to create the mobile enhancement culture is potentially a worthwhile topic of investigation.

Morphing Mobiles

The cultural icon status and attraction of the mobile phone has spread well beyond its consideration as a communication tool. It is now a highly prized status symbol, especially among the pre-teens and teens. Certainly this is recognized by marketers in a variety of domains (as well as humorists who poke fun at the preoccupation).

Just like other fashion items, the mobile phone has become an aesthetic object that people adopt and modify according to their sense of self and group affiliation. Like other fashion items, they use the device to project a sense of identity and self into public arenas. However, in order to perform self-presentation with the mobile phone appropriate to the particular culture or social group, users need to be attuned to the cultural meanings of the mobile phone, especially in an age that some marketers have dubbed "brand-morphing." ("Brand-morphing" refers to the way meanings of brands change across various social or cultural groups, Kates and Goh, 2003). The data presented here suggests that not only meanings of certain brands but also meanings of certain mobile phone designs are in the process of "morphing." At least to a group of people who are conscious about the style of the mobile phone, the phone is not a mere tool for convenience, but an expression of identity (Katz and Aakhus, 2002).

Consumers of the mobile phone often not satisfied merely to adopt the culturally appropriated meanings presented by the industry. They themselves attempt to "morph" the meanings of the mobile phone in various creative manners. Phones with expensive jewelries or the models that appear in popular movies are not the only "fashionable" phones.

Three lines of process can be identified. These are (1) co-locating the mobile phone in the commercial space of another product in order to use the status of the mobile phone to promote that other product; (2) creating products that can be used to enhance the appearance (but not function) of the mobile phone or personalize it to reflect the user's identity; and (3) users creating their own craft products to fill the conceptual space of the mobile.

In terms of the first line, the image of the mobile phone has been used to cross-market a variety of products. On the one hand, it has been used to attract interest to a product. For instance, in 2003 a McDonald's "Happy Meal" container included on the one panel alone three images of a cell phone including one of Ronald McDonald using the mobile phone. (see figure 5.3) In 2004, Bacardi was using a universal travel charger for mobile phones as a "gift-with-purchase" to promote sales of its new lemon-flavored rum.

On the other hand, products can be designed to look like or mimic mobile phones. Examples of such items in my personal collection include baby bottles, key chains, and make-up kits. Particularly interesting, from the notion of melding fashion and mobile communication, is an eye-shadow make-up kit which was designed to simulate a mobile phone. The make-up kit is styled to look like a sleek, small mobile phone and is visually attractive in its aquamarine color. Quite realistic looking, without careful examination it has in my experience fooled many casual observers who were surprised that it folds out not into a working phone but rather a selection of eye-shadows.

In terms of the second line—enhancements—a large secondary market or so-called "after-market" has developed. This includes utili-

Figure 5.3
Side Panel of McDonald's "Happy Meal" Container

tarian items, including headsets and carrying pouches. It also includes more personal items, such as photo-booths that serve as vend-
ing machines to produce adhesive photos for gifts. Often these are
co-branded, such as with Hello Kitty stickers or pasted-on photos,
antenna ornaments, and, most especially, custom covers and shells,
play an important part in fashion displays of mobile phones.

Another form of enhancement is "mobile phone morphing" which
can occur by the well-thought-out strategies of the industry. It arises
from the mobile makers' attempts to offer new shells, varieties, or
configurations of models. It also occurs through the intervention of
third parties or "after-market" manufacturers. Many examples may
be seen dangling in shops and markets around the world. But one
instance among my own collection is a mobile phone earphone/

microphone combination featuring a smiling kitty reflecting cuteness reminiscent of the "Hello Kitty" phenomenon (Belson and Bremner, 2003).

Folk Reinterpretation

A third line of morphing is folk reinterpretation. In response to professionalized production, artisans and crafts people create their own enhancements. For example, a student of mine returned from her trip to Namibia in 2001 with a hand-carved wooden mobile phone (figure 5.4). She had purchased it at an outdoor market. It is marked with a Sony brand name, and this artifact was made long before the Sony-Ericsson partnership, so there was no Sony branded mobile phone yet in existence. Was it a toy? Perhaps. At the same time, there was in the 1980s and 1990s a vigorous market for pretend antennas that could be attached to cars, giving onlookers the impression that the car-owner had his or her own car phone.

Figure 5.4
Hand Carved Namibian Mobile Phone

There are also a variety of handmade objects, often sold in markets throughout the world. Examples that have been drawn to my attention include items from both the developed and developing world. For instance, hand-carved mobile phone holders, made from mahogany, are sold in Morocco, and in India there are sold handmade silk purses purpose-built for carrying one's mobile. In the U.S., similar items are sold at local flea markets.

So, taken as a whole, the evidence appears strong that the creation and consumption of mobile phones becomes a multi-party process. However, it should be apparent that style and appeareance are often important in the way the mobile phone is understood by users and audiences alike.

Anti-Images

A main theme of this chapter has been the way commercial promotions of cell phones use certain themes and images. However, it is also useful to bear in mind that these images can serve as a framing point to oppose the technology. This aspect of image and subgroup solidarity was discussed in Apparatgeist theory (Katz and Aakhus, 2002). The theory draws our attention to the way images of mobile phone promotions can frame the anti-uses and forms of resistance. Subculture values may be questioned by the ads, which mean that those who support those values will be forced into opposition. So it can be helpful to understand as well the way resistance is formed to mobile phones as a technology and to the companies that invoke lifestyle symbolism.

This process may be illustrated by a report in 2005 that authorities in Bangladesh had requested that TV channels not air "indecent" mobile phone advertisements. In the predominantly Muslim country, the ads on behalf of GrameenPhone were perceived as promoting vice. Officials objected to scenes of young people playfully chasing one another and having "meaningless chats," according to press reports. The ads were described by an information ministry official as "not decent," and as using language and gestures that are "not consistent with the country's culture and values." Broadcasters were told that the ads might "promote the youth to immoral acts." (In response, a representative of the agency behind one of the ads commented that it was designed for young people "who are smart and up-to-date.") (Agence France Presse, 2005).

Figure 5.5
Handcrafted Ceramic Salt & Pepper Shaker

Another anti-image arises from humor. Bumper stickers are sold with the phrase, "Hang up and drive!" Cartoons in newspapers often pillory the mobile phone-obsessed. In a different take, a pair of handcrafted ceramic salt and pepper shakers has been made. These are made by a U.S. artesian (figure 5.5). The expressions on the figurines' faces suggest less than pleasure at being permanently connected to a mobile phone. The dry humor of these works of art and household amenities suggest a droll resistance to the proliferation of mobile phones.

Conclusion

This chapter analyzed fashion forms and personalization of the image of the mobile phone. What I have sought to add with this analysis is a more precise connection between an industrial ethos (marketing a futuristic status symbol) and the popular reception and co-creation of a communication technology. Moreover the folk artistic aesthetic and uses have become socially significant aspects of mobile phone consumption. Folk culture and artistic endeavors have added new layers of meaning to the mobile phone. In this way the mobile phone becomes not only a communication tool but also (depending on circumstances) a status symbol and individual value statement. It is every bit as much of a fashion statement as the choice of one's clothes. And just as the choice of clothes could include secular as well as sacred garb, so too the "fashion" statement of a mobile phone can be used for purposes ranging from the temporal to the transcendental.

This analysis is at variance with theories of mass society, and of cultural studies of oppression, both of which traditionally tend to suggest that the consumer is easily gulled by large corporations. We find instead a rich weaving of unexpected uses, form modifications and novel additions.

Of course, the mobile phone *qua* decorative endeavor is not a universal impulse; many users just accept the mobile phone as an "off-the-shelf" item. They find the phone to be neither of inherent interest nor intrinsic beauty. They also refrain from use and display when others are about. But while these types of people do exist, there also appears to be vast numbers of mobile phone users who are heavily fashion conscious. Many users invest the communication object with myriad personal decorations and also personal significance.

No broad-based statistical evidence can be pointed to as to the prevalence and consequence of these outlooks. Rather, here I have presented evidence to suggest that many consumers find mobiles to be a technology that fits extremely well with their values and interests, and which they adopt in droves. Nevertheless, users are more than mere consumers. They are also co-creators. They achieve this status by further manipulating mobile devices after purchase to reflect personal tastes and to represent themselves to the outside world. As in the case of audience reception theory, mobile phone users are like audiences of various mass media texts, creating, interpreting, appropriating material, to develop meaningful, personalized, and culturally appropriate new texts. As such the technology is present in both front stage and backstage social processes. The mobile phone then may be seen not only as a "necessary accessory" to the body, as Fortunati (2002: p. 58) has argued. It also becomes a communication device that reflects and embodies the user, and is used to communicate effectively with the physically present audience, passive though it may be, as much as the distant interlocutor, as ethereal as it may be.

Note

This chapter is based on, Bodies in motion: Industrial design and folk art in public mobile communication, with Satomi Sugiyama. In Rich Ling and Per Pedersen (eds.) *Mobile Communications: Re-negotiation of the Social Sphere*. Surrey, UK: Springer, 2005, pp. 57-83.

References

Agence France Presse (2005). Bangladesh asks television channels not to air "indecent" adverts. August 30, 12:04 PM ET http://www.suntimes.co.za/zones/sundaytimesNEW/basket11st/basket11st1125551568.aspx

Belson, Ken and B. Bremner (2003). *Hello Kitty: The remarkable story of Sanrio and the billion dollar feline phenomenon*. New York: Wiley.

Bormanis, A. (undated). Features: An interview with Andre Bormanis. Startrek.com. Retrieved from www.startrek.com/startrek/view/ features/firstperson/article/3840.html

Crane, Diana (2000). *Fashion and its social agendas: Class, gender, and identity in clothing*. Chicago: University of Chicago Press.

David, Kalpana (2004). Gender and mobile phones: A cultural investigation. New Jersey Communication Association Annual Meeting, April, New Brunswick, NJ.

Davis, F. (1992). *Fashion, culture, and identity*. Chicago: University of Chicago Press.

Fischer, Claude (1992). *America calling: A social history of the telephone to 1940*. Berkeley, CA: University of California Press.

Fortunati, Leopoldina (2002). Italy: Stereotypes, true and false. In James E. Katz and Mark A. Aakhus (Eds.), *Perpetual contact: Mobile communication, private talk, public performance*. Cambridge, Cambridge University Press, pp. 42-62.

Fortunati, Leopoldina, James E. Katz and Raimonda Riccini (Eds.) (2003). *Mediating the human body: Technology, communication, and fashion*. Mahwah, NJ, Lawrence Erlbaum Associates.

Goffman, Erving (1959). *The presentation of self in everyday life*. New York: Anchor.

Goffman, Erving (1974). *Frame analysis: An essay on the organization of experience*. New York: Harper.

Goffman, Erving (1979). *Gender advertisements*. New York: Harper.

Haddon, Leslie (2003). "Domestication and Mobile Telephony." In James E. Katz (Ed.) *Machines that become us: The social context of personal communication technology*, New Brunswick, NJ: Transaction Publishers, pp.43-56.

Hafner, K. (1999). A designer who sets a worldwide standard for technophiles, *New York Times*, December 09, p G.1. Retrieved from ProQuest electronic database.

Himmelstein, Hal (1993). *Television myth and the American mind*. Second edition. Westport, Connecticut: Praeger.

Kaiser, Susan (1997). *The social psychology of clothing* (Second edition). New York: Macmillan.

Kates, S.M. and C. Goh (2003). Brand morphing: Implications for advertising theory and practice. *Journal of Advertising*, *32*: 59-69.

Katz, James E. and Satomi Sugiyama (forthcoming). Mobile phones as fashion statements: Evidence from student surveys in the U.S. and Japan. *New Media & Society*.

Katz, James E. and Mark A. Aakhus (Eds.) (2002). *Perpetual contact: Mobile communication, private talk, public performance*. Cambridge, Cambridge University Press.

Leung, Lance and Ran Wei (1999). The gratifications of pager use: Sociability, informa-tion-seeking, entertainment, utility, and fashion and status. *Telematics and Informatics*, *15*: 253-264.

Leung, Lance and Ran Wei (2000). More than just talk on the move: Uses and gratification of cellular phone. *Journalism and Mass Communication Quarterly*, 77(2), 308-20.

Marvin, Carolyn (1988). *When old technologies were new: Thinking about electric com-munication in the late Nineteenth Century*. New York: Oxford University Press.

Massaris, P. (1997). *Visual persuasion. The role of images in advertising*. London, Sage Publications.

Motorola (2003). Motorola célèbre les 20 ans du mobile: Dossier de presse, 17 Juin 2003. Retrieved from *http://www.motorola.com/mot/doc/0/637_MotDoc.pdf*.

Motorola (2004). New York City Elite Flip Over the New Motorola A630. Retrieved from www.motorola.com/mediacenter/ news/detail/0,,4413_3747_23,00.html.

Oehmke, T. (2004). The hot phone. *New York Times*, 11.14.99. pg. SM74. Retrieved from ProQuest electronic database.

Oksman Virpi and Pirjo Rautiainen (2003). Extension of the hand: Children's and teenager's relationship with the mobile phone in Finland. In Fortunati, Leopoldina, James E. Katz and Raimonda Riccini (Eds.) (2003). *Mediating the human body, Technology, commu-nication, and fashion*. Mahwah, NJ, Lawrence Erlbaum Associates, pp 103-12.

Pajnik M and L-T Petra (2002). Observing discourses of advertising: Mobitel's interpel-lation of potential consumers. *Journal of Communication Inquiry*, *26*: 277-299.

Rakow, Lana (1992). *Gender on the line: Women, the telephone, and community life*. Champaign, IL: University of Illinois Press.

Reuters Singapore (2004). Diamante mobile phones anyone? *Taipei Times*, April 20, p. 16. Retrieved from *http://www.taipeitimes.com/News/feat/archives/2004/04/20/2003137447*.

Selingo J (2004). The cellphone: A new joy of childhood. *International Herald Tribune*, March 20, p. 18. Retrieved from Gale InfoTrac electronic database.

Snellman S (2003). A movie can be the best commercial. *Helsingin Sanomat*, Business & Finance—February 04. Retrieved from http://www.helsinki-hs.net/news.asp?id=20030204IE2.

Stein, S. R. (2002). The "1984" Macintosh ad: Cinematic icons and constitutive rhetoric in the launch of a new machine. *Quarterly Journal of Speech*, *88*: 169-192.

Swartz, K. (2003). Style ranks high in cellphone design. Knight Ridder/Tribune Business News, Nov 10. Retrieved from InfoTrac electronic database. ITEM03314009.

Swett, C. (2002). Cell-phone accessories market booms as devices become fashion state-ments. *The Sacramento Bee* (CA); September 01. Retrieved from EBSCO electronic database.

Wei, Ran and Victor Lo (2003). Staying connected while on the move: Cell phone use and social connectedness. Paper presented at the 53rd annual conference of International Communication Association, San Diego, CA, May 25-28.

Zhang, Y. B. and J. Harwood (2004). Modernization and tradition in an age of globaliza-tion: Cultural values in Chinese television commercials. *Journal of Communication*, *54*: 156-172.

6

Mobile Phones in Educational Settings

Recent Changes in Classroom Environments

Because people adapt rapidly to change, participants and observers sometimes have difficulty noticing alterations in prior routines and environments. Is it possible, for instance, that the school classroom has changed more in last few years than it did in the preceding hundred?

Physically, today's classroom is similar in layout and process to the classroom of twenty or even a hundred years ago. Blackboards still dominate. Despite many predictions since the 1950s, television only supplements lectures and has not supplanted them. The Internet has not inspired students to study science and math by looking at virtual laboratory benches and chatting online with researchers. Although students turn heavily to the Internet for doing research, writing papers, playing games, and chatting, it has generally not much altered the atmosphere of the classroom—something that even students have criticized (Trotter, 2004), except perhaps to add a distraction.

Video cassette recorders, compact disc recorders, networked computers, and computer software have wrought some changes in classroom settings, but another digital technology may be forcing a change in the dominant paradigm of classroom-based education. Today more than one out of three people worldwide are mobile phone subscribers, and mobile telephones, digital cameras, personal digital assistants (PDAs), and laptops that are enabled with wireless fidelity (WiFi) are seemingly omnipresent.

Both local and global dimensions of change have been brought together in the classroom in novel ways. A culture of perpetual contact has come together with a loss of a sense of place and a potential for amusing ourselves to death: students now easily communicate with the world beyond the classroom and engage with nearly endless entertainments and distractions (Meyrowitz, 1985).

Control of the Educational Environment

For some philosophers of education, students must be within controlled environments to learn successfully, and education should inculcate information, values, and behavior into the minds of others (Scott, 1970; Katz, Stevens and Vinovskis, 1987). These "total institutions" use coercion, denigration of the self, uniforms, and physical demonstrations of respect for authority to control the individual (Goffman, 1961). They limit contact between individuals within the institution and between insiders and outsiders. In kindergarten through twelfth grade (K-12) schools, for example, hall passes are typical, and uncontrolled communication is frowned on. Public phones are generally near the principal's office, but communication from outside the classroom typically are one way and local—via public address announcements. Of course, mobile devices are changing this situation, as will be discussed below.

The Initial Reaction: Ban Mobile Technologies from Schools

Although the Internet generated positive speculation about its potential effects on education, the mobile phone was identified as a source of irritation, delinquency, and even crime. Initially, school authorities banned pager and cell phone use inside school buildings to prevent them from being used for selling drugs or organizing gangs. In the United States, at least twenty states banned their use in K-12 public schools. (Some exceptions, such as is the case with a 1988 California law, were made for medical necessity.) These early policies did not emerge from thoughtful technology assessments, and mobile phones were not integrated into the school curriculum.

Today the Los Angeles school district and many others continue to ban the use of pagers and cell phones (Hefland and Hayaski, 2003) but state laws against them have largely been abandoned because of safety concerns, especially after the school shootings in Columbine, Colorado, on April 20, 1999, and the terrorist attacks in

New York, Pennsylvania, and Washington, D.C., on September 11, 2001. Parents also have pressured school authorities to allow mobile phones in schools for their convenience in coordinating school and after-school schedules. As one mother in Texas said of why she approved of having her daughter take the mobile to school: "We've had lockdowns at school before and she text-messages me to let me know what's going on. She also calls to tell me when she needs to be picked up or where she's going" (Critchell, 2005).

The Adoption of Mobile Technology by Young People

Prominent examples of research on mobile phones and young people include Leopoldina Fortunati's path-breaking studies of Italy (Fortunati, 2001) and Rich Ling's authoritative investigations (2004). Students of all ages seem to feel pressure from many "social engineering" sources to adopt mobile phones—from ad campaigns, from product placements in TV shows, films, and entertainment events, and even from parents (Chaisri, 2001).

Some academic experts advocate giving mobile phones to ten- and eleven-year-olds. In 2001, professors at the University of Gloucestershire found that about half of the 351 primary school pupils they surveyed had phones and that 38 percent had used their phones in a crisis situation (one out of seven also had sent a "frightening" message to a student). They concluded that lack of ownership could "harm social development and learning and lead to negative self-feelings and isolation." (Charlton, Panting and Hannan, 2001: p. 162). Another researcher disagrees: "Cell phones don't contribute to learning. . . . There are no good reasons for children to have cell phones" (Sherman, 2002).

Teens in Scandinavia and parts of Asia have near 100 percent mobile phone ownership. A 2004 survey found that 47 percent of U.S. students age twelve through nineteen carry cell phones. (A 1999 poll found that only 10 percent of young people from thirteen to seventeen years had cell phones.) Another 2004 survey of eight- to ten-year-olds found that 29 percent owned a cell phone (up from 18 percent in 2002) and that for eight- to ten-year-olds the mobile phone is "as much a status symbol as a communications device" (Selingo, 2004).

I was unable to find current national data about cell phone adoption rates among U.S. college students. One survey of mostly nineteen-year-old students (N = 421) at Rutgers University found that rates of adoption were 98 percent. Based on my own informal discussions with students from Taiwan, Korea, and Japan, rates among students in these countries are high.

The Usefulness of Mobile Phones in Educational Settings

What are the pedagogical consequences of this tidal wave of technology that breaks longstanding arrangements of control and hierarchy in schools? Mobile technology is working with education in several ways. One way is as a form of tutoring. Wireless application protocols (WAP) that use cell phones to access the Internet help users find definitions and reference information while on the move. A U.S. publisher, for instance, supplements its business textbooks with mobile phone-supported educational services such as flashcards, key terms, and self-quizzes (McGraw-Hill Higher Education, 2004). Executives of the firm said, "Many students today have complicated schedules and need to maximize small increments of free time. Knowing this, we recognized the need for delivering flexible ways to study materials outside of the classroom" (McGraw-Hill, 2004).

Mobile phones connect students with teachers and other students and help them deal with class attendance issues, rearrange meetings, retrieve schedule and assignment data, discuss assignments, coordinate study groups, and seek help with academic and life problems.

Cell phones also help teachers manage their own schedules more effectively. In an experiment conducted in a large Texas school district in the early 1990s, twenty-five itinerant teachers of children with visual disabilities were given mobile phones. Researchers— who investigated time-management efficiency, costs, changes in use patterns for both wired and wireless phones, and teachers' feelings of security—concluded that the technology was highly cost effective, increased teachers' feelings of security, and improved their communications with parents, other professionals, and schools and base offices (Corn and Patterson, 1994).

Administrators can delegate many time-consuming, repetitive tasks to mobile phones. At Korea's Sookmyung University, students use mobile phones to confirm attendance, enter libraries, buy food in the school dining hall, and prove identity (Sookmyung Women's University, 2004).

Mobile devices can allow parents to monitor their children remotely. This can help kids get to their appointments on time and reduce parental anxieties about their children's whereabouts. A location-monitoring service at a Korean school allows parents to confirm the location of their child within a school environment.

In 2005, a big step was taken towards giving timely and fine-grained information about students to their parents. In Croatia, the education ministry, working with an indigenous company, deployed an SMS alerting system in more than 100 schools. The system sends reports about children's school achievements and attendance to parents via SMS text messages. These reports include details about the children's school achievements and attendance, as well the children's behavior and marks. Also included are reports of absences and performance of homework assignments. According to one school administrator, "If a child does not appear in school the parent will know within ten minutes" (AFP, 2005).

Student Attitudes and Behavior

Some authorities feel that student use of mobile phones is a positive development. A developmental psychologist has said, "By using technology, children are feeling more of a sense of mastery and are feeling good about themselves" (Trotter, 2003). Adoption behavior certainly shows that U.S. students are using mobiles in colleges, high schools, middle schools, and even elementary schools.

A Pew Internet and American Life Project poll (N = 1,162) found that one-third of college students play video games on their cell phones and laptops during class. Respondents said that their academic performance was not affected by these practices (Gilroy, 2004), a claim that needs examination.

Rough comparisons can be made with other countries. A 2002 survey (N = 1,682) of Norwegian students who were mostly between sixteen and eighteen years old found that three-fourths of respondents said they were supposed to have their mobiles turned off during class. Interestingly, about the same percentage said that they had their mobiles turned on during class. In fact, 91 percent of the students reported reading during class SMS texts they had received and 84 percent said they had sent them during class (Berit Skog, personal communication). A 2003 Korean survey of middle and high school students (N = 497) found that 45 percent of schools controlled the use of mobile phones but that 68 percent of their students used mobiles in class anyway. About 41 percent of students reported that they had been disturbed by another's use of a mobile phone (Sung Nam Citizen Committee, 2003).

At Rutgers, we surveyed a class of information-technology students who were mostly twenty years old (N = 221). Half had used a mobile phone during class in the preceding week to check for calls or messages (41 percent), to be distracted from a boring class (34 percent), to answer calls (29 percent), to talk to a friend (23 percent), to find out what a friend was doing (23 percent), and to download (6 percent). About half found others' use of phones in class to be distracting. Only 4 percent of students thought that it was all right to speak into a phone in class, but they also thought that text messaging (45 percent) and game playing (30 percent) were acceptable.

In response to a question about mobile phone addiction, one out of seven students said that they felt addicted to their phones. This sense of addiction may correspond with dependency and heavy usage.

Our survey also yields interesting clues about the social contagion aspects of mobile phone use in class. About 44 percent of respondents agreed that if one student begins using a phone in class, others will use their own phones.

An Experiment

Reports show a pattern of intense in-class use of mobile communication technology—to overcome ennui, to display a high-status item, and to perform functional or social tasks. It is not uncommon for students (and others) to say they could "not live" if they did not have their mobile phone (Katz, 2003).

To investigate this dependence and understand the role played by mobile phones in their lives, we invited students to participate in an experiment to refrain from cell phone use for forty-eight hours. The goal was for participants to appreciate (and describe for researchers) the role of mobile technology in their lives. Of the 102 students solicited, eighty-two participated in the experiment, and twelve finished the experiment (a mortality rate of 85 percent) (figure 6.1). Students said that they failed to finish the experiment because it was too hard, urgent issues arose, people got angry with them, and responsibilities required them to use their phones.

We also asked students how their lives were different during the two-day hiatus. Three respondents said that their life was happier without a mobile phone; 70 percent disagreed with this view. The mobile phone seems to have migrated from a luxury to a "necessary luxury" (in Fortunati's phrase) and finally to a vital communication tool.

Figure 6.1
Levels of Participation in a 48-Hour Experiment to
Forego Mobile Phones, April 2004

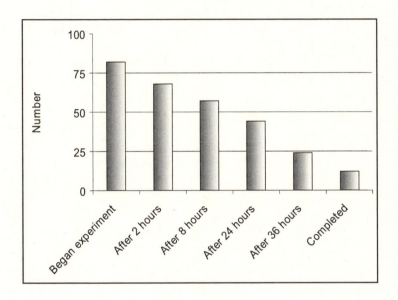

Some Behavioral Dimensions of Mobile Phone
Use in the Classroom

News stories about mobile phone use by students in educational settings suggest a variety of problems, including disruption of class, delinquency, chicanery, and erosion of teacher autonomy.

Disruption of Class

In 2002, a pizza deliveryman arrived at a Virginia high school with an order for a student who had ordered the pizza because he had missed lunch. Commented an astounded principal: "He didn't see anything wrong with it" (Lee, 2992). A Connecticut principal reported that an eighth-grade boy "boldly took out a cellphone during history class and ordered a pizza." The principal reprimanded the student and confiscated the mobile phone. Scrolling through the phone's recently called numbers ("looking for numbers of known drug dealers"), he discovered that the boy "had called my house six times in the middle of the night. My wife and I remember the hang-ups vividly" (Mooney, 2003).

There is also at least more than a theoretical chance that any teacher who seeks to control mobile phone use in the classroom runs risk of physical injury. A female lecturer at a college in Saudi Arabia was injured when an angry female student assaulted her. The student's assault "was provoked by the lecturer's repeated demand to shut off her mobile phone while in the lecture hall" (Al-Anazi and Al-Faleh, 2001).

Delinquency

In 2001 in Great Britain (I could not find comparable data for the United States), about 28 percent of robberies involved taking a mobile phone, and about 700,000 mobiles were stolen—nearly half from children under age eighteen (figure 6.2) (BBCi, 2002a). Some thefts occurred during a mugging or a violent attack that resulted in a knifing or death, and about 1,000 victims were twelve years old BBCi, 2002b). Moreover, bullying among children can be exacerbated by mobile phones (Pacienza, 2004). (They also can help alleviate it.)

Chicanery

Mobile communication devices have been used for chicanery in educational settings, especially for truancy and for cheating on tests. Truants have had students inside a school building use mobile phones to tell them when to return to avoid detection.

A teacher in California reports that a student showed her a cell phone picture of a test question that had been sent to him by another student in the class (Mobile Youth, 2004). A University of Maryland professor posted a bogus answer key on the Internet after a test had begun. By comparing students' answers with the bogus answer key, the teacher uncovered a dozen cheaters, who appeared

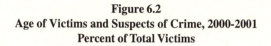

Figure 6.2
Age of Victims and Suspects of Crime, 2000-2001
Percent of Total Victims

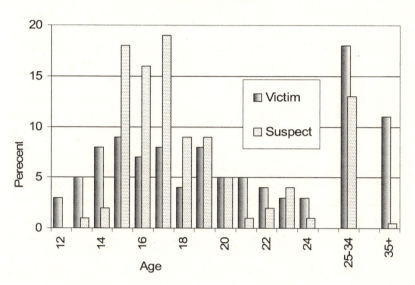

Source: Home Office as reported by BBCI, 2002. (Does not add to 100 due to rounding errors.)

to have independently had friends send them answers from the key (Manning, 2003).

Similarly, a Tokyo university failed twenty-six students (out of about 500) for cheating on their e-commerce final exams when a student left the classroom during the exam and sent his classmates e-mail messages containing answers. Professors noticed that these students produced identical answers, including mistakes (Chronicle, 2003; Brown, 1998; Argetsinger, 2003).

Erosion of Teacher Autonomy

Teachers have required students to leave phones outside test settings. At the University of Maastricht, "mobfinders" make a beeping sound when they detect mobile phone use in their vicinity. University officials anticipate that alerting students to the possible use of the device might eradicate the practice (Reinhardt, 2001).

In spring 2003, the National Education Association asked members of its higher education division if professors should ban cell phones in their classrooms, and 85 percent answered yes (Gilroy, 2004). About 74 percent of California's secondary school principals support a ban (Helfand and Hayasaki, 2003).

Some teachers enforce rules that govern classroom mobile phone behavior. In a 2002 course syllabus, a social psychology professor at the University of New Mexico-Albuquerque included this notice:

> Turn off mobile phones when in class. I do not want to hear your phones ringing. If your phone rings, I will ask you to leave class immediately and not to return until the next class. If it keeps happening, I will ask you to drop the course. The only exceptions are if you have a child or other dependent for whom you have to remain available in emergencies; if so, please let me know this is your situation in advance (i.e., send me an e-mail before the second class meeting, August 22), and get a phone with a silent vibrating call alert rather than an audible ring. [Underscoring in the original] (Miller, 2002)

A systematic approach is outlined in a syllabus for a cellular biology class offered at a Massachusetts technical college:

> Students can remain in the course until they have accumulated 10 points, at which time they will be removed from the course. Absence from class or lab, coming to class or lab late, and leaving class or lab for extended periods of time count as 1 point each. Interruption of class or lab by a mobile phone or beeper also counts as 1 point. (Tamarkin, 2004).

Some teachers strike back directly at phone calls that disturb their classes. One professor takes a ringing phone and asks the caller to add to the class discussion. She reports that after one episode of this kind, her students seldom let their phones ring during class time (Marklein, 2003).

Students are not the only ones who disrupt class with mobile phones. One interviewee reported that her daughter's third-grade teacher regularly took personal calls during class, which led administrators to ban the practice. In a 2004 survey, nearly two-thirds of 100 Rutgers students reported that their professors had taken calls during class. In fact, I witnessed a professor receive a call during a lecture and leave the room to discuss a medical condition with his physician.

To explore the issue a bit further, in early September 2004 I asked some questions of a class of Rutgers undergraduate students (most of whom are about twenty years old, and two-thirds of whom are female), about their cell phone habits and experiences, especially as related to classes; the figures are presented in table 6.1. To begin, it is noteworthy that nearly all had cell phones: of the fifty-three students in class, all but 1 reported having a mobile phone and the one student who did not said he had owned a mobile previously but currently was unable to afford one. Of those having them, the majority (73 percent) had their mobile phones on during the class, even while the survey was being taken. Of the thirty-eight who had them on during class, 13 percent said that they had received a call or message since the class had begun, that is in preceding twenty-five. No sounds were heard by me, and the students all said their phones were on vibrate mode. (It is worth bearing in mind that U.S. students are much heavier users of voice services than SMS services.)

Perhaps even more interesting is the fact that about half of the students indicated that they had witnessed a professor taking a mobile phone call during class. This proportion of students, who have observed such behavior, unsurprisingly, seems to continue upward as the technology becomes more widespread, more commonplace, and as the elapsed years of experience increase.

Several examples of this were discussed among the class members. One incident revealed how a professor had lectured his students about the importance of not having the cell phone sound during class. The next week, his mobile phone began sounding. He took the call for a moment, and then apologized to the class. Other professors were more extensive in their use of the mobile phone during class, including engaging in arguments with their spouses. In another illustration, this one from 2003, a professor of information science received a call during a doctoral seminar. He excused himself from the room, saying the call was from a doctor whom he had been trying to reach for an extended time period. That left the students baffled as to what they should do until the professor returned several minutes later.

Although not subject of the college-level survey, it is worth reporting an event that transpired which was an even more extreme example of teacher misbehavior. This took place in an elementary school in December 2003. It was reported that a music teacher of fourth-grade students (that is, children who were about ten years old) engaged in protracted discussions of up to five minutes long during class time. He would go over to the classroom's windows to

get better reception; meanwhile the bored students would begin tri-
fling. In less extreme examples, another fourth-grade teacher would
excuse herself and tell the students that the call was related to her
wedding planning.

Table 6.1
Student Experiences with Mobile Phones in Educational Setting

Experience	Percent
Have mobile phone with them at present	98
Have mobile phone on during class [silent or ring mode]	73
Received phone call during the first 25 minutes of current class	10
Recently made call/sent text message in another class	19
Have seen their teachers use mobile phone during class	49

N=53, percentages rounded; survey September 9, 2004

One implication of this small-scale investigation is that the classroom is no longer the isolated learning environment that it once
was. Rather it is blending into the rest of the life, creating an environment of perpetual contact. As mobile games proliferate, the
trend towards "outside interference" will continue. Certainly it is
worth considering how educational processes will unfold when
all students and teachers are fully equipped with mobile communication devices.

Consequences of Mobile Phone Communication for Education

Mobile phone communication benefits education on at least three
levels. Operationally, it makes class management, including attendance and administration, easier and more effective. On the time-
management level, it enhances coordination between teachers and
students. Finally, it provides students with greater access to course
and supplementary educational resources.

On the other hand, mobile communication activities in classrooms
have negative aspects, including cheating, harassment, and delinquency. Additional problems may also be emerging, including dam-
age to attention spans, critical-thinking skills, and respect for learning and teachers. Students who are distracted lose the ability to con-

Note

hapter is based on, Mobile phones in educational settings. In Kristof Nyiri (Ed.)
se of Place. Vienna: Passagen Verlag, 2005, pp. 305-19.

References

rance-Presse (2005). Text messages to keep tabs on Croatian schoolchildren.
nber 2, 2005. Retrieved from *http://www.physorg.com/news6205.html*

, Fayadh and Hussein Al-Faleh (2001). Seven teens given 15 lashes each for
ing women. *Arab News*, May 17. Retrieved from *http://www.arabnews.com/
=1&section=0&article=1951&d=17&m=5&y=2001.*

er, Amy (2003). U-Md. says students use phones to cheat; text messaging
rs test answers. *Washington Post*, January 25, p. B1.

02a). Huge surge in mobile phone thefts. *BBCi* website, January 08. Retrieved
ttp://news.bbc.co.uk/1/hi/uk/1748258.stm#only.

02b). Teenager stabbed for mobile phone. *BBCi* website, June 12. rretrieved
ttp://news.bbc.co.uk/1/hi/england/2040337.stm.

arah Mae (1998). Russian students turn the page on cheating. Ethics: collegians
scow state university use cellular phones and beepers to get answers to exam
ons; one professor even praises their initiative. *Los Angeles Times*, April 26, p.

eeraporn (2001). Parents glad to give kids cell phones. *The Nation* (Thailand),
ry 29. Retrieved from Gale InfoTrac electronic database.

Tony, Charlotte Panting, and Andrew Hannan (2001). Mobile telephone owner-
nd usage among 10- and 11-year-olds: participation and exclusion. *Emotional
ehavioral Difficulties* 7(3): pp. 152-163.

e of Higher Education (2003). Japanese students caught in cellphone cheating
" *Chronicle of Higher Education*, January 03, p. A44.

ie L., W. Patterson, C. Love and J. N. Erin (1994). The use of mobile telephones
tinerant teachers of students with visual disabilities. *Journal of Visual Impair-
nd Blindness*, 88 (5): pp. 446-457.

Samantha (2005). Schools try to find balance on back-to-school gadgets. Asso-
Press, August 02. Retrieved from *http://www.suntimes.com/output/education/
-btsgadgets21.html.*

, Leopoldina (2001). "The mobile phone: An identity on the move," *Personal
biquitous Computing 5*: 85-98.

, Leopoldina (Ed.) (1998). *Telecomunicando in Europa*. Milan: Franco Angeli.

arilyn (2004). Invasion of the classroom cell phones. *Education Digest 69*(6):

Erving (1961). *Asylums*. New York: Doubleday.

Duke and Erika Hayasaki (2003). L.A. Unified to study campus cellphone ban.
ngeles Times*, September 23, p. B1.

es E. (Ed.) (2003). *Machines that become us: the social context of personal
unication technology*. New Brunswick, NJ: Transaction Publishers.

chael, Edward Stevens, Jr., and Maris A. Vinovskis, (1987). The origins of
high schools. *History of Education Quarterly 27*: 241-258.

ifer 8 (2002). As Gadgets Go to Class, Schools Try to Cope. *New York Times*,
t 15. Retrieved from http://mathforum.org/epigone/mathedcc/zholalchend.

centrate, to plan, and to work with comp
and sometimes seem to reflect a general d

A Death-Knell for the Cl:

Mobile communication technologies intr
ing confusion" (in William James's memor
teachers seem to accept more easily thar
parts. Public school authorities do not ha
overcome parental and student resistance t
ban, when in an era of both local and glob
this technology as a lifeline to their child
transmogrified into an entitlement. It cann
but it can be controlled (even though sm:
will be harder to detect).

Mobiles are further accelerating change
way—fostering student autonomy while en
ment, helping parents affect how classes ar
dren are doing even as they are more dist:
ing greater monitoring of and accountabi
over, the predictions of advocates of "di
students are physically dispersed but men
turned on their head. Instead, students m
even while being physically present.

By allowing students to defect from th
pursue their own concerns or amusements,
classroom to become as much about enter
pline. In some ways, when the "here and
cally present group are sacrificed for the
who are distant in space and time, perso
public norms.

The image of schoolchildren staring ou
minds preoccupied with daydreams, could
students staring forward—not daydreaming
brating gadgets, chattering with offsite frie
rials from outside the classroom. Tomorr
may be the perfect tutor in the local/glob:
futurologists anticipate.

This
A Se

Agence
Sep
Al-Ana
hara
?pag
Argetsi
deli
BBCi (.
fron
BBCi (
fron
Brown,
at M
que
13.
Chaisri
Janu
Charlto
ship
and
Chroni
scar
Corn, A
with
men
Critche
ciat
cst-
Fortun:
and
Fortun:
Gilroy,
56-(
Goffma
Heflanc
Los
Katz, J.
com
Katz, N
pub
Lee, Je
Aug

Ling, Richard S. (2004). The mobile connection: The cell phone's impact on society. San Francisco: Morgan-Kaufman.

Manning, Stephen (2003). University of Maryland students admit to using cell phones to cheat. January 30. Retrieved from http://www.signonsandiego.com/news/computing/20030130-1331-cellphones-cheating.html.

Marklein, Mary Beth (2003). Hanging up on class disruptions. *USA Today*, October 29, p. D5.

McGraw-Hill (2004). McGraw-Hill/Irwin Announces Innovative Pilot Study Tool on Cellphones: Study to Go for Cellphones Offers Next Generation of Mobile Student Tools. Retrieved from http://www.prnewswire.com/cgi-bin/stories.Pl?ACCT=104&STORY=/www/story/04-12-2004/0002149565&EDATE=.

McGraw-Hill Higher Education (2004). Retrieved from http://www.mhhe.com/business/cellphone/images/phone3.html.

Meyrowitz, Joshua (1985). N*o sense of place: The impact of electronic media on social behavior.* New York: Oxford University Press.

Miller, Geoffrey (2002). Syllabus for Social Psychology 271. Retrieved from http://www.hbes.com/HBES/syllabus-miller-socpsych.htm.

Mobile youth (2004). Retrieved from http://www.mobileyouth.org/news/mobileyouth1258.html, 2004.

Mooney, Thomas B. (2003). Legal mailbag. *CAS Bulletin* (Connecticut Association of Schools) (February). Retrieved from http://www.casciac.org/legal_mailbag/feb03.pdf.

Pacienza, Angela (2004). Proliferation of e-mail, IM makes cyberbullying common activity among youth. March 20. Retrieved from http://news.yahoo.com/news?tmpl=story&u=/cpress/20040320/ca_pr_on_tc/the_cyberfile_1.

Scott, Donald M. (1970). The social history of education: Three alternatives. *History of Education Quarterly 10*: 242-254

Selingo, Jeffrey (2004). The cellphone: A new joy of childhood. *International Herald Tribune*, March 20, p. 18. Retrieved from Gale InfoTrac electronic database.

Sherman, Thomas (2002). Thomas Sherman, professor of education, quoted in Cell Phones Don't Contribute to Learning. Virginia Polytechnic Institute and State University, public release dated July 12, 2002. Retrieved from http://www.eurekalert.org/pub_releases/2002-07/vt-cpd071202.php.

Sookmyung Women's University (2002). The Hankyoreh: Introduction of "mobile campus" [original in Korean], August 26. Retrieved from http://www.hani.co.kr/section-005100006/2002/08/005100006200208261404059.html.

Sung Nam Citizen Committee (2003). Research on use of mobile phones in high and middle schools in Korea. Retrieved from http://www.chosun.com/w21data/html/news/200312/200312260261.html.

Tamarkin, Dawn (2004). "IOL351-D01: Cell Biology. Syllabus. Retrieved from http://distance.stcc.edu/cellbiology/syllabusS04.htm.

Trotter, Andrew (2003). Students' technology views solicited. *Education Week*, October 15, p. 1. Retrieved from *http://www.b-g.k12.ky.us/Tech/StudentsTechnologyViewsSolicited.pdf.*

7

The Telephone as a Medium of Faith, Hope, Terror, and Redemption: America, September 11

with Ronald E. Rice

Introduction

The twenty-first century was supposed to have been, as Francis Fukuyama famously declared, the end of history. Instead, a defining historical deflection occurred due to the terrorist attack of September 11, 2001 on the United States of America. The topic of this chapter is the way people used the telephone and related technology to address their situation and needs during the terrorist assault on New York City and Washington.

A Syntopian Perspective

Ronald E. Rice and I developed a theoretical perspective that we call "Syntopia." The term Syntopia is derived by combining the Greek terms "syn" and "utopia," which means "together place." It thereby signals a new synthesis of various media and social interactions, and the erosion of the distinction between (technologically constrained) one-on-one communication, typical of the wireline telephone, and mass media, typified by television and commercial radio. Instead, we have new media technologies that combine both systems, and allow the user to migrate quickly from one to another (or find new ways of mixing them or adding new functionalities, such as location-based services). In this way, we see technology as able to foster increased connections among people and within communities. The term also includes not only a positive note, but also recognizes the obvious dark side of new media. This is reflected in the homophone "sin," which alludes to the possibility that mediated communication can be exploited for evil and harmful purposes, even ones that are inadvertently so (Katz and Rice, 2002). In essence then, the new technology, especially synthesized through various media combinations, can provide communication that is richer and more controllable, diverse, and real seeming than traditional face-to-face communication. It certainly allows greater customization and fulfillment of individual desires. The question that remains to be answered is how well and to what effect it can fulfill these previously existing and newly created desires, especially in terms of their larger social consequences (Rice, 1999).

The Syntopia perspective emphasizes the human uses and social consequences of telecommunication technologies in modern society. It avoids a mandatory ideological perspective (whether it be historical determinism, post-modernism, or technological determinism) and instead, embraces an empirical-pragmatic tradition.

Propositions about September 11 Telephone Use Based on a Syntopian Perspective

We have organized our analysis around eight propositions implied by a Syntopian perspective.

1. The telephone allows intense immediacy.

Shortly after the attack began, someone who answered the phone on the trading floor of broker Cantor Fitzgerald, whose offices were near the top of World Trade Center 1, was asked what was going on. He said, "We are fucking dying!" (Reuters, 2001). Rocco Medaglia, a contracting supervisor, was completing a job on Tuesday morning at Cantor Fitzgerald's offices in Tower One. "Just making sure everything was as it should be," said his daughter, Ms. Diana Medaglia. Minutes before Tower 1 collapsed, the Medaglias received in quick succession three phone calls. The family thought the calls must have been from a trapped Rocco. "We couldn't hear anything on the other line but we hope that he could hear us, so we just were yelling into the phone," his daughter said. Shortly after each call, the line would go dead (Williams, 2002). Mr. Medaglia also perished.

2. Contact and reassurance communication with primary social group members is among the highest priority in emergency situations, and may endure across time and space.

For many, letting others know they were loved by their special someone was their highest priority, and they tried to accomplish this by any communication means possible. Last words: We who are about to die love you. Many other messages of love and concern were sent out across land-line, mobile phones, pagers, and the Internet that day. Declarations were not frilly, fancy, or creative. They were terse and conventional. But they were also extraordinarily meaningful.

Lee Hanson's son (Peter), his wife (Sue Kim Hanson), and their two-year-old daughter (Christine) were killed September 11 when their flight, United Flight 175, crashed into the World Trade Center. Peter, thirty-two, used his cell phone to call his parents in Easton, Conn., moments before his plane hit the second tower in the World Trade Center. "The fact that he called me—he could have called any number of people," Mr. Hanson said. "I take a lot of comfort in that. He thought enough to do that" (Associated Press, 2001b).

The telephone also allowed a mother and daughter to share their last minutes together. In the case of Ms. Olabisi Shadie Layeni-Yee, the situation on September 11 was doubly poignant. Ms. Layeni-Yee had been working at the World Trade Center in 1993, when it was bombed by terrorists. Ms. Layeni-Yee's mother had watched that event unfold on television, but had no idea what was going on with her daughter. Hours dragged by as the event was covered live on local TV. Finally, she got a call from her daughter. "Mom, I'm fine"; she had been helping a pregnant woman walk down from the seventy-ninth floor. On September 11, things were different. On that morning, the mother's phone rang. It was her daughter. She urged her mother to turn on the TV, then quickly told her the situation, concluding with the words, "If worse comes to worst, I'm just calling to say goodbye to all of you." Then she told her mother that the lights were going out and the floor was buckling. The mother turned around quickly towards the TV screen; it was a long shot of the tower collapsing (Clymer, 2001).

The telephone answering machine and voice messaging allowed some to receive a message that they would otherwise have missed, and has continued to give enduring meaning and a sense of emotional immediacy to the lives and relationships that were destroyed that day. Shortly after September 11, a reporter called the number of a victim's family. A telephone answering machine picked up his call. The pleasant-sounding woman's voice explained that Ian and Christine can't take the call, please leave a message. The reporter commented that Christine will never be able to take the call, as she too was killed by the hijackers. Trying back later, he reached Christine's husband, Ian Pescaia. Mr. Pescaia said he had not intentionally left the message on the machine. He explained to the reporter, "I haven't had a chance to go get another tape....It's just the only tape. And I didn't want to erase it" (Roddy, 2001).

3. Communication technologies, separately and in combination, were used to seek information and reassurance and to establish contact with loved ones.

Adam Mayblum was in Tower 1, which was struck by the first aircraft. His office, which was below the point of impact, lurched back and forth ten or more feet. No one dreamed an airplane had struck their building but rather thought a bomb had gone off. He, like others, thought the worst was over. Like many others in an emergency situation, his thoughts turned to his family. He relates,

> My wife had taken our 9-month old for his check up. I called my nanny at home and told her to page my wife, tell her that a bomb went off, I was ok, and on my way out. We were moving down very orderly in Stair Case A. Very slowly. No panic. At least not overt panic. My legs could not stop shaking. My heart was pounding. Some nervous jokes and laughter. We checked our cell phones. Surprisingly, there was a very good signal, but the Sprint network was jammed. On the phones, one out of 20 dial attempts got through. I knew I could not reach my wife so I called my parents. I told them what happened and that we were all okay and on the way down. Soon, my sister-in-law reached me. I told her we were fine and moving down. I believe that was about the 65th floor. We were bored and nervous. I called my friend Angel in San Francisco. I knew he would be watching. He was amazed I was on the phone. He told me to get out, that there was another plane on its way. I did not know what he was talking about. By now, the second plane had struck Tower 2. We were so deep into the middle of our building that we did not hear or feel anything. We had no idea what was really going on. We kept making way for the wounded to go down ahead of us." (Mayblum, personal communication, 18 September 2001)

Note that Mr. Mayblum and those around him, though in the bowels of the WTC in New York, only got the first inkling of what had happened by talking by mobile phone to someone in San Francisco.

4. Transmission of both information and affect are highly important, and users may be extraordinarily sensitive to nuances, regardless of the medium.

In terms of coordination and alerting, Tom Burnett, aboard the doomed United Airlines flight above Pennsylvania, used his mobile phone to both alert his family and the authorities. When he reached his family, who lived in a suburb of San Francisco, his wife, Deena, was in the middle of making breakfast for their three girls. The call took her aback, and Tom sounded odd, she thought. She asked, "Are you OK?" "No," was his reply. Speaking in a quick, low voice he said, "I'm on a plane, it's United Flight 93, and we've been hijacked. They've knifed a guy, and there's a bomb on board. Call the authorities, Deena." Then he hung up (Breslau, Clift, and Thomas, 2001).

The BlackBerry and other handheld wireless e-mail devices, like two-way pagers, served as lifelines to friends and loved ones and workmates, and as a way to stay in contact with the office. People without hearing were able to use their mobile technology for text-based communication to reassure friends around the world in the midst of the horror. Susan Zupnik had been deaf from birth, wanted her mother to hear her voice on that fateful day in September. She and Carl Andreasen, thirty-seven, both deaf employees of the Port Authority, were breakfasting in a cafeteria on the forty-third floor of the North Tower. "Suddenly, my face was thrown against a window," Zupnik told a reporter. She then saw debris falling down outside the windows. People were screaming around her, but she could hear nothing. . . ."I threw my bagel on the floor and ran out," she says. Ms. Zupnik had an AOL Mobile Communicator, a device she purchased only months earlier. It allows her to send and receive messages. She keyed in a message to a friend, an administrator at the New Jersey Institute of Technology, that something was wrong. Then she received a news bulletin over her pager—a plane had hit the World Trade Center. As she slowly made her way down the stairs, the communicator buzzed constantly. Friends from all over the world—in California and Maryland and Ireland and South Africa and England—were asking whether she was safe. "I'm on the 26th floor," she punched on the tiny keyboard to answer one concerned note, and continued her escape (Braun, 2001).

5. Use of telecommunication technology leaves important residues that reveal complex communicative interactions.

Using new media inevitably leaves residues, because the modern telecommunications infrastructure involves many computers, with associated store-and-forward capacities and with complex abilities to track message flow for billing, routing, and system optimization purposes. For example, we have pictures of some of the hijackers using ATM machines, going through airport security, and entering newsstands. Or, they can continue to represent potential interactions. News outlets carried hopeful stories that perhaps someone with a mobile phone could call for help from under the rubble, or even if the individual were unconscious, the mobile phone could still generate signals that would enable rescue. One journalist who traveled to Ground Zero on September 11 said that firefighters reported that the eeriest sound of all was mobile phones and pagers ringing underneath the debris as loved ones still frantically tried to find and contact those missing. (O'Dowd, 2001)

6. New social relationships and arrangements emerge around the use and non-use of new media.

When people find themselves confronted by disaster they will usually band together, overcoming pre-existing social barriers. In studies of telephone service breakdowns, people share their limited resources, and turn to neighbors; friendships and community spirit develops (Katz, 1999). A young man relates how he and a previously unknown neighbor befriended each other as they stood on their Manhattan tenement roof watching events unfold: "After exchanging a few scant phrases of disbelief (after all, what could one say?), he invited me down through his window to use his phone. (Like most New Yorkers, mine was nearly useless for most of the day.) I called my mother back in Michigan." (Aldo, 2001). (Two-thirds of the voice lines in lower Manhattan that were cut after terrorist attacks on the World Trade Center have been re-connected by Verizon, but 100,000 lines are still without service, the telecommunications company said September 25, 2001. Most were business lines, though.) (AP online, 2001). Bill Singer, an attorney who was escaping ground zero by foot, noted scores of individuals milling about, sobbing. "They often held cell phones. They cried that they couldn't reach their husband, their brother, their father, their sister, their mother, their friends. And strangers would simply walk up to them, put their arms around them, comfort them." (Singer, 2001).

7. Users can be highly creative in developing ad hoc solutions and crossing media boundaries.

People are primarily concerned about the goals and processes of communication, not the technology. Thus people were creative in their use of available telecommunication technology to solve their immediate needs. When their first communication channel was blocked, they tried the next available alternative. If the plausible alternatives failed, they would begin cobbling together their own patchwork and fallback systems to get messages to loved ones, no matter how. For example, many sent Internet email messages asking recipients to phone others about the sender's situation. Or, consider one mother who was vacationing at "the Habitat" in Bonaire, when a friend ran to her group saying, "They're bombing America." A few moments of watching TV in the open-air bar panicked her, as she thought that her daughter might have skipped school and been shopping at Pentagon City. "Running for a telephone proved to be a futile proposition. There were simply no lines available. Instead, I bought a 45-minute Internet card and stuck myself at the Internet kiosk in the lobby at Habitat. While I was frantically emailing, the first tower of the World Trade Center imploded onto hundreds of rescue workers.. . . Within 10 minutes I got the answer I was waiting for from my ex husband. Morgan and everyone else I knew was fine. That information was priceless" (Barry, 2001).

8. Some people may seize an emergency as an opportunity to use communication technologies to attract attention to themselves, initiate harm to others, or symbolize the event.

The telephone, mobile phone and Internet of course enabled many things to take place that otherwise might not have happened on September 11, for both good and bad. Indeed, the attack on the World Trade Center was organized and implemented at least partly through mobile communication. The terrorists communicated with each other from one plane to another by mobile phone as they sat on the tarmac that fateful morning.

There were many reports of mobile phone messages being received from people trapped under the WTC. Unfortunately reports of this nature were later shown to be spurious (Associated Press, 2001a). Although some of these reports to authorities were believed to be correct at the time by the callers, they were often caused by people's misunderstanding of signaling and confirmation records, and a few were malicious. One woman, Sugeil Mejia, was sentenced to three years in jail for leading rescue workers on a wild goose chase through the rubble of the World Trade Center. She had fabricated a story that her husband, who she said was a police officer, and ten colleagues, had contacted her by mobile phone from the depths of the rubble several days after the September 11 attack (Associated Press, 2002).

Many people began using their mobile phone to commemorate the September 11 incident, but not always in the way we would expect. In what was interpreted as an anti-American gesture, a graphic began circulating among mobile phone users in the Middle East. The message was described by the *Economist* as appealing to "terrorist sympathizers" throughout the Middle East. The simple graphic, which can be easily sent on the advanced phones commonly used in Europe and the Middle East, shows an airplane crashing into a skyscraper. The caption, in Arabic, was "It hit and did not miss" (*Economist*, 2001).

Conclusion

The particularly dramatic, tragic, and devastating event of September 11, 2001 provides many examples of how new communication technologies both represent and shape Syntopia—a dynamic social context where media are used for diverse human purposes, often in combination with other media, both intentionally and unintentionally, both in expected and unexpected ways, to communication both intense emotions and immediacy as well as objective command control information, for ill and for good. Our examples here have suggested a variety of propositions about new media—especially telephonic media—that emphasize aspects of communication that more traditional media theories have overlooked. The uses of telephone technology as a medium of faith, hope, terror, and redemption in the September 11 event are not determined by material forces, but by the interrelations among the uses and capabilities of society's media, and by the heart, spirit, and emotional and social needs of humankind.

Note

This chapter is based on, The telephone as a medium of faith, hope, terror and redemption: America, September 11, with Ronald E. Rice. In A. M. Noll (Ed.), *Crisis communications: Lessons from September 11*. Lanham, MD: Rowman and Littlefield, 2004, 83-98.

References

AP online (2001). Retrieved from http://www.nando.net/special_reports/terrorism/rescue/story/105408p-1202534c.html.

Aldo (No last name provided, 2001). Notes from a Brooklyn rooftop. Retrieved from http://stoozrecords.com/World percent20Trade percent20Center.htm.

Associated Press (2002). WTC Hoaxster sentenced to three years. Falsely claimed she received call from under WTC rubble. Retrieved from http://cbsnewyork.com/terror/StoryFolder/story_1629942698_html.

Associated Press (2001a). Terror hits home: Thousands feared dead as nation begins recovery from strikes. Retrieved from http://www.nd.edu/~observer/09122001/News/11.html.

Associated Press (2001b). Victim's father seeks help for others. Retrieved from http://www.gazettenet.com/americantragedy/09262001/6823.htm.

Barry, Mikki (2001). Retrieved from http://mystory.inter.net/browse.php?action=next&pt=0. Great Falls, VA.

Braun, Bob (2001). From the newsroom of *The Star-Ledger*. Newark, New Jersey. October 2. Retrieved from http://www.wels.net/pipermail/voice/2001October/000047.html.

Breslau, Karen, Eleanor Clift and Thomas, Evan (2001). The Real Story of Flight 93. *Newsweek*, December 03. Retrieved from http://www.msnbc.com/news/NW-WEBEXTRA_Front.asp?cp1=1.

Clymer, Adam (2001). The cord that bound them. *New York Times*. December 11. Retrieved from http://www.nytimes.com/2001/12/11/national/portraits/POG-11YEE.html.

Katz, James E. (1999). *Connections: Social and cultural studies of the telephone in American life*. New Brunswick, NJ: Transaction Publishers.

Katz, James E. and Rice, Ronald E. (2002). *Social consequences of Internet use*. Cambridge, MA: MIT Press.

O'Dowd, Niall (2001). An Irish Journalist speaks of Ground Zero. September 22. Retrieved from http://endtimespeculate.crosswinds.net/V.

Rice, Ronald E. (1999). What's new about new media? Artifacts and paradoxes. *New Media and Society*, 1(1), 24-32.

Reuters (2001). Four airliners used in terrorist attacks on United States. Reuters report. September 12, 12:00 am EDT. Retrieved from http://www.airdisaster.com/news/0901/wtc0912/news.shtml.

Roddy, Dennis (2001). Echoing voices of erased lives. *Pittsburgh-Post Gazette*, September 22. Retrieved from http://www.post-gazette.com/columnists/20010922roddy102col2p2.asp.

Singer, Bill (2001). The World Trade Center tragedy. Retrieved from http://www.singerfru.com/wtc.html.

Economist, The (2001). Hot leads, stolen identities. September 20. *The Economist*. Retrieved from http://www.economist.com/agenda/displayStory.cfm?Story_ID=789176.

Williams, K (2001). The lost. *Newsday*. Retrieved from http://www.newsday.com/news/local/state/ny-iethum2367639sep15.story.

Part 2

Telecommunication and Information in Society: Past, Present, and Future

8

The Telephone and Social Transformation

No technology has done more for more people yet been proportionately less studied than the telephone. This chapter seeks to assess the telephone in broad terms, a technology that has enormously extended the reach of the human mind.

Historical Development

The term telephone is based upon the combination the Greek words, *tele* ("distant" or "afar") and *phon* ("sound" or "voice"); it was first used in France in the 1830s as a name for a crude acoustic device. By the mid-1800s something akin to a pair of tin cans connected by a taut string was known in the United States as the "lover's telephone." In 1876, Alexander Graham Bell won a patent for a device which the world has come to know as the telephone.

In the telephone's early period, myriad uses were explored. Among them were "broadcasting" news, opera, weather reports, and religious services. Some contemplated services never materialized: A. G. Bell speculated that the telephone might be used to communicate with the deceased. Other services did not materialize because they were outdated before they could deployed: France's national phone company conducted substantial research in the 1960s to see if the telephone touch-tone pad could be adapted to serve as a home calculator.

Since its invention in 1876, the telephone has become an important aspect of everyday life throughout the industrialized world and, increasingly, the developing world as well. It is so commonplace that only its absence becomes noteworthy, such as during emergencies, when regular phone service is disrupted and even mobile phones cease working. Even domains that were formerly free of phones, or had their access to them sharply restricted, have become part of the broad fabric of telephonic communication. Once inviolable, beaches and mountaintops are now part of the "chatter-sphere." So too is it interestingly the case with school classrooms and prisons, which are often porous to telephone technologies. Too easily forgotten by laypersons and scholars alike is the miracle of (at least potentially) being able at any time to place a call to any other subscriber worldwide. The enormous value of the telephone can be appreciated if one only considers the plight of a villager who wants to know if there might be work available in a nearby town, or who needs to summon aid for a sick family member (Strom, 2002).

Also easily overlooked are the ramifications of this global connectivity. By allowing people to transcend a variety of physical and social barriers, the telephone has led to a complex set of dispersed personal and commercial relationships. By any measure, the telephone has dramatically altered the social landscape (Aronson, 1971; Ball 1968; Katz, 1999). Cars and airplanes were adumbrated respectively by horse-drawn vehicles and birds. Yet, in human imagination, the power of real-time interactive oral communication over great distances had been a power reserved exclusively for divine beings. Given this godlike power of the telephone it is little wonder that it has been one of history's most successful inventions. Little wonder, too, that some of earliest experiments with it were designed to ascertain whether the telephone could be used to communicate with the dead. (Perhaps not regrettably, the answer is that it cannot.)

Global and Micro-Coordination

For billions of people, the quotidian act of making or receiving a telephone call in their home or business or on the street or bus is often a normal occurrence. (Another billion or so, at the short end of the development spectrum, have in their entire lives never used a telephone.) For rapidly growing numbers of people worldwide, car driving and cityscape walking are becoming settings for making and receiving phone calls. Given the commonplace quality of the ordinary telephone it remains hard to delineate, let alone appreciate, the telephone's ramifications throughout global societies and the interior world of individual psyches.

Although the telephone has substantial cumulative macro-social consequences, most of them are predicated on its ability to support social interaction. An essential aspect of the telephone is its ability to allow coordination among geographically dispersed (or even locally concentrated) people. Numerous studies demonstrate that the telephone promotes business, sociality, democracy and information flow (e.g., Fischer, 1992). For those who are physically handicapped or otherwise constrained, it opens vast arrays of contacts. (It is interesting, and perhaps surprising to note that the telephone has greatly increased the social contacts and informational resources for the deaf, via TTY and short-message service (SMS) interfaces. This quality is particularly gratifying given Alexander Graham Bell's original interest in helping the deaf.)

The telephone allows convenient management over distance, and via voice messages and texting, asynchronously. Upon its basis, extraordinarily large enterprises can be established and effectively controlled. As a corollary, those who would otherwise have greater independence find themselves circumscribed by others (sometimes literally) above them. The telephone has enabled the rapid conduct of large-scale financial transactions and has greatly assisted the formation of capital markets.

A collateral effect is that digital telephonic technology, including mobile and voice-mail voice-mail systems, has been partly responsible for the elimination of huge numbers of middle managers and support staff throughout American industry. Ironically, many of these positions were created in the first place to deal with the communication flood created by the analogue telephone.

Answering machines and voice messaging, which, of course, allow the conveyance of telephone messages without human intervention. In former times, self- respecting managers, professors, or other professionals would be reluctant to conduct their business without having a secretary on staff. (Clearly much effort necessarily went into "faking" the existence of a secretary to act as an intermediary.) Today, for many professionals, having a secretary would seem to be not only wasteful but also an indication to their clients that they are out of touch with the best current practices. The dream of a robot secretary, expressed in the late nineteenth century seems to be coming into virtual existence in the twenty-first century.

The proliferation of digital messaging, including voice-mail and answering machines, also affects the tenor of professional events.

For instance, it used to be the case that at a conference or symposium, the breaktime would be used for social interaction and enjoying the "here and now" aspects of the conference venue. Nowadays, however, attendees rush outside the meeting chamber to use their mobile phones or flip open their laptops in an attempt to get their messages and email and return phone calls. They rejoin the world of "in touch," assuming they have somehow resisted the temptation of covert communication while in the meeting. In another context, the mobile phone and PDA (personal digital assistant) have led to a new form of social effrontery. While seemingly engaged in conversation, one coolly glances down and scrolls through messages on one's communication device, all the while nodding sagely as if heeding every word uttered by one's interlocutor. These are a few of the many faces of what Kenneth Gergen (2002) has termed "absent presence." People are seemingly at an event or socially engaged, but their attention and mental focus is elsewhere.

Telephones, especially mobile phones, increase the pace and efficiency of life. They also allow more flexibility and individual efficiency at business and professional levels and at those of family and personal life. Moreover, people can take action to allay the feeling they are not accomplishing enough. People can harness spare time, or time previously spent in tasks that do not require much attention (for instance, waiting on a shopping queue) to plan and coordinate with others, get information, or even shop remotely by phone while they also shop in person. On the other hand, those who treasure respite may find themselves pressured to replace otherwise excusable isolation with productive tasks. Once upon a time, being aboard an airplane excused an executive from having to interact with colleagues on the ground. No more, for messaging, faxes, and phone calls now follow even at six miles high; nor are funerals and religious services beyond their reach. An age of perpetual contact has dawned; the immediate future, for once, is quite clear. Many services that have been independent services, such as voice-mail, text, video, photos, video-conferencing, and email, will become unified and be presented to the user in a single "inbox" available from just about any location. Moreover, as compression techniques, data distribution resources, and frequency usage efficiencies advance and expand, ever-richer media will be readily available. This will allow individuals to have much greater control over their life activities, information resources, and personal contacts.

Despite the many advantages to having the telephone available any time and anyplace, there are drawbacks to it as well at both the individual and social levels. The telephone can be a minor irritant or a conduit for crime. In terms of the former, many social critics of the late nineteenth century expressed irritation at the way the telephone seemed to destroy the orderly pace of life, the considerable pleasures of social propriety and, as well, those of solitude and reflection; the target has remained lucrative, and the frustrations of telephone use and abuse remain a staple of folk and media discourse. The telemarketing solicitation, is also an oft remarked upon irritant. Telemarketers themselves use market research, so it is no accident that their calls seem to arrive at dinnertime or other exquisitely inconvenient moments. More serious, though, is that there are a large variety of swindles—some of which even use computer-aided dialing schemes—that prey especially on those with the fewest social resources. Stalking by telephone and obscene phone calls to both men and women are also serious problems. On the other hand, with advances in technology that give call recipients greater power to control access to themselves (such as popular caller-identification services) people are better able to mange their communication environment to suit their individual tastes and needs.

The increasingly nuanced technology available to callers and callees demands ever- greater sophistication to achieve a flawless performance of the choreography of communication. Think of the dilemma of a shy but sedulous teenaged boy who wants to ask a popular girl to the school prom. Presumably he would not want to leave on her caller-identification box a perusable record of his forty or so attempted calls before finally reaching her. The degrees of freedom and maneuver are reduced with intriguing consequences that cannot be explored here. Suffice it to say that, sadly, it appears that there is an iron law of telephone contact: people generally get the most calls from those from whom they would least like to hear, and vice versa.

In all, though at times a source of irritation and a conduit for criminal activity, the telephone has proven to be an important factor in increasing the pace, scope and intensity of business and management operations while simultaneously lowering the cost of engaging in these activities. It has had a parallel effect on people's levels of social interaction.

Geographical Distribution

The telephone has substantially influenced the distribution of people across the physical landscape. On the one hand, the telephone has allowed the massive vertical downtown urban center to come into being and thrive. Without the telephone, the skyscraper would have been most difficult to build and manage. Further, it would be difficult for the structure to maintain its usefulness to its denizens without the telephone.

Some claim that the telephone has enabled one particular form of geodemographic dispersion, the suburb. However, detailed studies of transportation-system development indicate that the telephone was not an important factor in this remarkable internal migration. Still, the telephone does allow many in rural locations to participate in business and social relations in a viable way, which without the telephone would not be possible. At the same time, those in extremely low-density areas have persistent difficulty getting even minimal telephone service; the situation is exacerbated by the fact that this population is generally poor and remote from economic opportunities. This, unfortunately, is a social problem that will endure for decades albeit diminishing over time, due to cell and other non-wireline technologies, including satellite-based ones. The telephone, though, has allowed those who choose isolation—and such people are often drawn from the middle and upper strata of society—to enjoy it without having to forego ready communication. Some seek to "get away from it all" but still want employment as consultants, or at least to stay in convenient contact with friends, family, and emergency services.

Economic Development

It has long been an article of faith that the telephone promotes economic development and social welfare. This belief has had powerful repercussions on national telecommunications policies worldwide. These have ranged from subsidized rates for the poor, subsidized rates for everyone, and special incentives for telephone companies to modernize their systems or physically extend their services to remote areas. Certainly there has been a strong association between telephone lines and economic growth, particularly, as Heather Hudson (1984) has shown, in developing countries. Researchers have demonstrated a logarithmic relationship between main telephone lines and national income on a per capita basis, although the direction of the causal arrow has not yet been established beyond question.

What is not in doubt is that the telephone itself fosters employment growth, not the least to serve itself as an industry. In the early days of mechanical switches, when telephone systems were growing dramatically, it was speculated that within a generation all young boys in America would have to be employed simply to connect phone calls. Although this scenario never materialized, phone companies have traditionally been enormous consumers of manpower, and are usually one of the largest employers of a region. Traditional telephone companies everywhere, though, are for the most part looking for ways to reduce their traditional workforces, heavily concentrated in jobs of installation or as operators. They are replacing vast numbers of these workers with smaller numbers of software engineers and technicians. Yet even as the workers per 1,000 telephone lines decrease worldwide, employment in the wireless telephone industry has mushroomed. In many cases, the growth in the mobile phone sector has far surpassed the cuts in the traditional wireline companies (many of which were formerly government ministries of Post, Telegraph and Telephone services or PTTs). As the expense of laying copper wire is far greater than erecting a radio tower, people are gravitating to mobile phones simply because they can get them more quickly and cheaply, and are often more useful, than wireline ones.

Telephones ease the job prospecting process directly, increasing economic efficiency by making it easier to find and change jobs. By using the telephone as a sales tool, consumption is stimulated, which leads to job creation and economic growth. Staffing the sales force alone of course means that jobs will be created. To illustrate by the situation in the U.S., according to the Direct Marketing Association, spending devoted to telephone marketing is about $62 billion annually and comprises nearly 40 percent of the nation's direct marketing expenditures. The telephone's indirect employment impact in telemarketing is substantial; in 2005, employment in telephone marketing was estimated at more than 4.25 million workers, according to the U.S. Direct Marketing Association.

Although much of the prior discussion focused on macro-economic effects, it is also worth mentioning the twofold micro-economic impact of the telephone. First, it allows individuals to run their own businesses, often from their home or voice mailbox. Thus, it encourages small enterprises. Yet, it also encourages large-scale enterprises as well since it allows firms to capture the benefits of large size without excessive coordination costs as discussed above.

Polity and Politics

Due to its ability to connect quickly with remote areas, the telephone has helped foster national integration. At a structural level, it also serves to centralize political authority while concomitantly circumscribing regional centers of power. Notwithstanding this structural aspect, the telephone has something of a reverse consequence for individual political empowerment. In this regard, Donald Ball (1968) and Sidney Aronson (1971) argue that the telephone has been a politically democratizing instrument. There is much to be said for this viewpoint, and studies have shown that, controlling for levels of economic development, in Communist countries of Eastern Europe there were equivalent numbers of television sets when compared to their Western European counterparts. However, there were drastically fewer telephones. The presumed reason for this mal-distribution is that the telephone enables two-way communication, whereas the television allows controlled information to be sent in a one-way direction from centralized source to a passive mass audience.

The important role the telephone system could play in controlling the populace has not been lost on governments. In the late nineteenth century, France wanted a centralized, governmentally controlled telephone system because authorities anticipated that rebels might otherwise be able to seize control of it during an uprising. Under the Soviet communist regime, the absence of telephone books in Moscow was legendary. Telephone tapping is a long-practiced art that has been used to fight crime and enemies of the state.

Revolutionaries as much as police recognize that the telephone is the nervous system of the body politic. Hence, it is the universal target for those seeking to subvert or protect the government. Lenin directed that the telephone and telegraph offices be the initial targets of his Bolshevik seizure of power. A contrary example in a parallel situation was the August 1991 coup attempt against Mikhail Gorbachev. The plotters failed to seize or block the telephone system save at Gorbachev's compound. Consequently, the anti-Communists were able to use their phones to rally resistance across Moscow and the republics. Boris Yeltsin and his supporters, barricaded in Russian government's "White House," were able to make and receive calls from around the country and the world, including U.S. president George Bush. It was said they even were able to phone in food orders to the local Moscow Pizza Hut (Russian.net, no date).

The telephone facilitates the management of political campaigns and the operation of political organizations. For well-organized campaigns, the telephone bank has become an important element in any contest. They can also be used to generate otherwise lethargic public interest in issues. In the United States, a neologism has been created to describe the abuse of this process. The term is "astroturfing," in honor of the artificial grass of the same name. Astroturfing is the process of using telephone banks to create the incorrect impression among politicians that there is a "grass-roots" swell of public concern about an issue when in fact there is little or none. Instead, the outpouring of opinion on the issue had been catalyzed by a small group of telephone operators who "pipe through" citizens to their representative's office to recite a prepared message. This example provides further demonstration of the principle that telephone technology has an impact that is governed largely by the motive of the user.

Societal Aspects

Traditional sociological variables of age, social class, socio-economic status, gender and race/ethnicity influence people's relationships with the telephone. Young people are generally much more likely to adopt new technology than are their older counterparts. Material resources, as measured by income, also have a noteworthy effect. Predictably, those at the very bottom of a society's income distribution are least likely to have telephone service. More surprisingly, as shown by my research (Katz, 1999), people in the third income quartile are disproportionately represented among purchasers of enhanced telecom services. One reason that would account for this finding could be that these services are perceived as entertaining or of high prestige. This surprising trend occurs in both Europe and the U.S.; whether it obtains in other regions is unknown.

Since its inception, there have been speculations about the small-group and social interactional consequences of the telephone. Carolyn Marvin (1988), in her path-breaking study of the social reception of the telephone (and other nineteenth-century electrical technologies), demonstrated that concerns over the impact of the telephone paralleled those of the larger society. Among these were the erosion of family authority, race and social class barriers, and sexual and social propriety. Also of substantial concern was disrespectful and deceitful behavior. Victorian-era Americans believed, justifiably, that the telephone reduced social cues ordinarily conveyed in the richer channels of face-to-face interaction and written correspondence. By masking cues, such as the location and social status of the caller, the telephone denied important cues to assist in making judgments about the interlocutor. Thus it would be easier to violate social and legal codes. These concerns remain substantial even after a century of telephone use and are born anew with contemporary communication technology such as the Internet.

The telephone plays a role in the conduct of gender relations and in the pursuit of sexual gratification. In contemporary, often-suburbanized society, the telephone has become an important means by which teens socialize themselves, build and sustain their relationships, and amuse themselves in a historical period when they are defined as problematical non-adults. Commonly, women run the "social work" of maintaining family links and social schedules via the telephone. (*Ceteris paribus*, when both a man and a woman are in a room together, a woman is twice as likely to answer a ringing phone.) Lana Rakow has documented the important role the telephone plays in women's friendships, and the ways it lends support for their independence despite various constraints and provides them with social resources they need to pursue their relationships and goals.

As in other areas, the telephone can enhance coordination in people's search for partners. The telephone's role in abetting prostitution has long been noted. (The term-of-art "call-girls" clearly refers to the role of the telephone.) While it is impossible to capture precisely the temporal, economic, or organizational magnitude of the telephone's role in the commercial sex industry, plainly large sections of the Yellow Pages and of urban newspapers are devoted to presenting this information in a slightly hidden argot to knowing patrons. Phone booths in many countries are littered daily with miniature handbills enticing customers to one service or another.

The telephone can also serve as a less direct conduit for sexual expression. Almost by definition, the conduct of remote interactive sex is an entirely *de novo* mode of expression enabled by the phone. The remote as well as the disembodied aspects of a telephone call can have its sexual appeal, and in this regard one hardly need mention the candlestick design that characterized phones for a half century. It can also serve as a safe and sanitary substitute for in-person sex. Recognizing this pent-up demand, an entire industry of "pink services" has sprung up in any country where it is allowed. Definitive data as to its size are difficult to obtain, but a dataset from Austria is illuminating. Phone sex had historically been forbidden by Austrian law. However, in 1991, a revenue-sharing arrangement was established so that offshore companies could benefit from premium international telephone tariffs. The Dutch Antilles became a center of one such operation, and numerous companies began placing ads in Austrian newspapers giving their Antillean numbers. The results were dramatic and instructive. For all of 1990, the total duration in minutes of calls to the Dutch Antilles from Austria was exactly 13,050. For the first nine months alone of 1991, the number of minutes of calls from Austria to the Dutch Antilles exceeded 1,600,000 (Latzer and Graham, 1994). A similarly rapid growth in "adult content" is expected to occur in the area of multimedia services for mobile phones (Richtel and Marriott, 2005).

Not all telephone sex is predicated on a financial arrangement. Many millions of obscene calls are annually reported to authorities. Both men and women make obscene phone calls to obtain erotic stimulation from the reaction of their shocked victims. These types of calls seem to occur throughout the world wherever a telephone system is present. As a case in point, within a mere six months after the first automatic telephone network was installed in Papua-New Guinea, an obscene phone call was reported to authorities.

A third class of sexually oriented telephone calls is neither commercial nor inflicted on victims, but rather is by mutual consent. For decades, lovers have enjoyed erotic phone conversations, and the topic receives substantial treatment in literary and cinematic formats. Nevertheless, seldom has public attention to this private aspect of human behavior risen to the heights it did in 1998. As part of a larger relentless investigation, an incident of sexual gratification via telephone between U.S. president Bill Clinton and his White House aide, Monica Lewinsky, was given protracted national media attention and related to Congress in an official report. Thus presidents and perverts alike serve to demonstrate that the telephone, as every other communication technology—from the video camera to the car, and from the printed book to the web-enabled mobile phone—can be used by people as a context for sexual excitement and fulfillment. Sexual and romantic activities are also proliferating due to the abilities of the mobile phone services, especially those that pair up interests and allow location-based communication and contact.

Another striking aspect of the telephone is its use as a tool of personal empowerment. With emergency phone boxes set up on campuses, and especially with the mobile phone, people can feel safer in public places. It has expanded the locales and times that people, especially women, can go, thus increasing people's freedom and mobility. It also permits parents to expand the privileges they give their children in terms of when and where they can go. This has the intriguing result of both increasing and loosening parental control.

The telephone also enhances individual autonomy by allowing people to live more successfully by themselves. Yet it preserves instant access between those experiencing a medical or police emergency and a variety of support services. In addition, a substantial variety of community and psychological services are available at any hour and often with complete anonymity.

As with any technology, the use to which it is put is influenced by the motives of the human user. Just as not all people are good, neither are all purposes to which the telephone is put benign. The telephone has offered new venues for monitoring individuals, invading their privacy, and harming them materially or psychologically.

In terms of monitoring, the wireless revolution, particularly as it intersects with the telephone, is increasingly affecting all aspects of social interaction, from the conduct of relationships to the receipt of medical care. These technologies will not only be used to deliver services but also to monitor individuals. In the past, telephonic monitoring has targeted parolees and the elderly. The number of citizens who are regularly and passively tracked will be increasing; this will be done through the data collected by systems used to regulate mobile phones and so-called intelligent highways. Already mobile phone records are being used in civil (e.g., divorce actions) and criminal cases (e.g., the apprehending of kidnappers).

The telephone also gives individuals tremendous powers to affect others' lives at a distance. Though often used in pranks and practical jokes, the telephone has also been used to inflict protracted harassment and terror on others. Such practices include spreading malicious rumors, making harassing calls late at night, and even concocting identities in order to manipulate or frighten someone. In one case, a young girl pretended to be a nurse who reported (falsely) to another girl that her lab test results indicated that she had AIDS and was pregnant. The girl victim attempted suicide. Disaster was only narrowly averted when the culprit was caught by using caller-ID.

Coordination can be effected over great distances and barriers. This may be seen in a 2001 prison revolt in Brazil, and perhaps give an ironic meaning to the term "cell phone." On February 17, a coordinated revolt broke out in twenty-nine jails. The revolt, that lasted more than a day and involved about 20,000 inmates, led to at least nineteen deaths. The simultaneous uprising was organized by prisoners using mobile phone from their cells. Although not officially permitted in the jails, relatives of inmates claimed that it was easy to pay a bribe to get a cell phone delivered to any prisoner (Osava, 2002). The possibility of using cell phones to detonate improvised bombs is, unfortunately, all too well known.

Turning our attention to the underpinnings of social life, Claude Fischer found that a social-psychological effect of the telephone was that it seemed to accelerate the pace of social life. His classic study, *America Calling*, found that the spread of the telephone in the U.S. reduced isolation and increased social contacts. A concomitant finding is that a good proportion of telephone users experienced anxiety or "communication apprehension." Many citizens also feared excessive social contact, becoming the subject of telephone gossip, and being subjected to unwanted calls. However, he found no support for more extreme claims that it brought people to a constantly heightened sense of alertness and anxiety over the potential summoning outcry of the telephone's ringing bell. Fischer concludes that the telephone cannot be implicated and the emergence of "psychological modernity," that is, the contemporary sensation of free-floating anxiety and dehumanization. Rather, he concludes that people easily assimilated the telephone into their lives. They used it as "the conscious product of people employing things, not of things controlling people."

Technological Convergence

It is impossible to speak of today's telephone exclusively in its formerly traditional wireline configuration. Mobile phones, as discussed below, are but one aspect of this telephonic reconfiguration; it extends to all aspects of voice communication. One salient aspect is the way people manage their calls. For instance, in the U.S., a large portion of residential telephone subscribers also have some form of answering machine. This device changes how people use their phones, e.g., to monitor before picking up the receiver, and which in turn affects the behavior of the caller ("I know you're there! Come on, pick up."). Having the telephone answered by a machine was, until 1987, seen by the majority of the U.S. population as an act of rudeness to callers. It was emblematic of the fear that "robots would take over," and that people were losing control over their daily lives. (This also ties into the above point about the importance of having a secretary to handle one's calls.)

Still, the answering machine/voice mail is but one of the ever-multiplying ancillary service that are being added to the formerly black "one-size-fits-all" telephone. These include built-in faxes, caller-ID, three-way calling, call-waiting, and call-trace; together they are changing what a telephone is and how it is used, as well as the subterfuges that are used to work around the telephone's expanded capabilities.

Even as the telephone becomes more powerful and capable, it is becoming tetherless. Not only is the home phone increasingly likely to be cordless with reception to a 1/2-kilometer from base, but people are increasingly subscribing to mobile telephone services that will allow them to range across continents. Moreover, some people are abandoning their wireline phones entirely; in the U.S., about 7 percent of subscribers have done so already and their numbers are increasing. Among other things, this trend means the loss of geographical meaning to area codes. Mobile telephones are also becoming Internet enabled, further erasing the distinction between phone and computer. Although currently most users access the Internet via the computer, it seems inevitable that soon the majority will also be doing so from enhanced mobile phones. Computers themselves are increasingly encompassing the features of the telephone, becoming Internet phones and answering machines and voice-chat messaging. Personal digital assistants are beginning to act as both mobile phones and portable computers and in fact disappearing into them. Platform capabilities are becoming intermixed, that is, telephone conversations can occur virtually anywhere with anybody via any machine. One consequence of this technological advance is that, without too much hyperbole, it appears that there is arising a new sense of "perpetual contact." This new state will allow better coordination, improved business operations and enhanced kin and social relations. It will also introduce new conflict over the appropriate norms for, and possible constraints on, people's public behavior. To cite an instance, there may be set aside mobile phone-free subway cars and restaurant sections. And already there are laws against using mobiles during theatrical performances, and house rules about use of mobile phones while waiting in line or dining in a restaurant.

While some of the conflict revolves around manners and appropriate levels of sensitivity, the larger issue of the use of mobiles and individual conduct in public places is only beginning to be addressed. It remains an unsolved puzzle for social scientists and the architectural profession to create public spaces that can amenably co-exist with privatizing mobile telephonic behavior. However, the much more powerful issue is the question of safety. Mobile phones mean not only that lives can and will be saved but also that—because there are those who elect to use it while driving—lives will be lost. Sadly, there is a rising toll of people killed by mobile phone-using drivers. Those who are affected by such tragedies will be fostering legislation to restrict the use of mobile phones in cars.

The Telephone as Synecdoche for the Modern Condition

The telephone has had substantial impact on the structure and quality of human existence, from business to sex, and on the conduct of war and peace from the international to the intra-family level. Never has so small a device been used so easily by so many to do so much to so many.

The use and abuse of the telephone encapsulates and expresses the dimensions of social scientific perspectives on modern life. What happens on the larger canvas of life is reproduced within the ambit of life on the telephone. The telephone's impact stems from the inherent qualities of a technology that allows easy, inexpensive real-time interaction by voice over both short and great distances. People have aggressively investigated and exploited this technology's potential. Through this unrelenting effort, there has been an isomorphism between what the technology can achieve—as its capabilities become more sophisticated—and the needs and desires that exist within mankind's biological and social framework.

The telephone system has been used in ways as broad as the human imagination, and in ways that were never envisioned (or were even actively opposed) by telephone company system designers and marketers. Telephone systems have been used to broadcast operas and provide wakeup, dial-a-joke, and dial-a-prayer services. Psychological and emergency services, astrological advice, and interactive matchmaking services are among its staples. Users themselves have created a variety of "work-arounds" to beat the telephone system (e.g., tone-generating boxes that allowed callers to by-pass toll mechanisms). None of these uses or innovations were foreordained. Rather, as shown by Jonathan Coopersmith (1991), far from a calculated manipulation of telephone company executives, some innovations as enormously successful as the fax and answering machine were at various points in their development opposed and thwarted by telephone company executives.

Certainly, in an age of increasing perpetual contact, the telephone can seem like a dictator. Yet despite the frustration with too much supervision, in the main the telephone has become a servant to those pursuing profit and pleasure. The picture after more than a century and a quarter is quite unlike those sketched originally by hand-wringing dystopians such as Mark Twain. These critics saw the technology as depleting social capital, killing social relationships, and inducing depression (a view similar to today's critics of the Internet).

On balance, the telephone has clearly done far more to liberate humanity than to enslave it. This observation is not meant to downplay the harm that can be and is inflicted and inspired by the telephone. Like two other communication technologies—the airplane and the automobile—the telephone can be used for both good and evil, to aid or to thwart. It can be used to wreak havoc and misery or bear messages of love, hope and redemption across the neighborhood street or vast ocean. But as the Bible and the Greek myths remind us, even the divine must endure frustration.

Note

This chapter is based on, The Telephone. In Neil J. Smelser and Paul B. Baltes (Eds.) *International Encyclopedia of Social and Behavioral Sciences* Pergamon, Oxford. 2001, pp. 15558-65

References

Aronson, Sidney H. (1971). The sociology of the telephone. *International Journal of Comparative Sociology*. 12 (September): 153-67.

Ball, Donald W. (1968). Towards a sociology of telephones and telephoners. In Marcello Truzzi (Ed.). *Sociology and Everyday Life*. Englewood Cliffs, NJ: Prentice Hall, pp. 59-75.

Coopersmith, Jonathan (1991). The failure of the fax: When a vision is not enough. *Business and Economic History* 23 (1) (fall): 272-82.

Fischer, Claude (1992). *America calling: A social history of the telephone to 1940*. Berkeley, CA: University of California Press.

Gergen, Kenneth J. (2002). The challenge of absent presence. In James E. Katz and Mark A. Aakhus (Eds.), *Perpetual contact: Mobile communication, private talk, public performance*. New York: Cambridge University Press, pp. 22-241.

Hudson, Heather. (1984). *When telephones reach the village: The role of telecommunications in rural development*. Norwood, NJ: Ablex Publishing.

Katz, James E. (1999). *Connections: Social and cultural studies of the telephone in American Life*. New Brunswick, NJ: Transaction Publishers.

Latzer, Michael and Graham Thomas (1994). Cash lines: The development and regulation of audiotex in Europe and the United States. New York: Springer.

Marvin, Carolyn (1988). *When old technologies were new: Thinking about electric communication in the late Nineteenth Century*. New York: Oxford University Press.

Pool, Ithiel de Sola (Ed.) (1977). *The social impact of the telephone*. Cambridge, MA: MIT Press.

Osava, Ario (2002). Simultaneous riots in Brazil prisons leave 15 dead. Asheville Global Report. Retrieved from http://www.agrnews.org/issues/110/worldnews.html

Rakow, Lana F. (1992). *Gender on the line; Women, the telephone, and community life*. Champaign: University of Illinois Press.

Richtel, Matt and Michel Marriott (2005). Ring tones, cameras, now this: Sex is latest cellphone feature. *New York Times* September 17. Retrieved from http://www.nytimes.com/2005/09/17/technology/17porn.html.

Russianet.ru. (undated.) Retrieved from http://www.russianet.ru/~oldm/history/coup.html.

Strom, Georg (2002). The telephone comes to a Philippine village. In James E. Katz and Mark Aakhus (Eds.) *Perpetual contact: Mobile communication, private talk, public performance*. Cambridge: Cambridge University Press, pp. 274-283.

9

Accounting for Information in Society

My purpose here is to review major schools of thought concerning information in society, or more precisely, the information society. The topic is of substantial importance to scholars as they struggle to understand the processes and implications of information creation, processing, and assimilation. I begin by looking at the meaning of the term information, and how it has been used and interpreted. Some policy and ethical issues related to information are discussed, and some ironies of information are observed and commented upon.

Analytical Approaches

Information may be considered on three different levels: (1) uncertainty reduction; (2) patterned abstraction; and (3) knowledge. The term itself connotes the recognizing, creating, encoding, transmitting, decoding, and interpreting of social patterns—in a word, communication—and often involves technology in some way. Information may also be considered at a meta-level: how and for whom the information is created, to what uses it may be put, and with what consequences.

By creating, modifying, and framing information, people can use information to alter the opinions and actions of others, and thus future states. Archaeological and ancient textual evidence demonstrates that an enduring concern of rulers and sages alike has been the crafting of messages to achieve desired effects. Aristotle and other ancient Greeks systematically analyzed the social context of information construction and delivery as well as its anticipated effect, including how various groups might be served or disadvantaged by its forms of public presentation. Many ancient elites, perhaps as much as modern ones, realized that information exists not as an essence but within in a context.

Yet despite this enduring thread in information use and analysis, modern concepts of information have a strong empirical and quantitative basis. In contrast to rhetorical analyses of the social applications of information, Paul Lazarsfeld's empirical studies of information transmission among groups must be considered foundational (Lazarsfeld, Berelson and Gaudet, 1944). He held that there was a two-step flow in interpersonal influence related to political opinions, with local opinion leaders playing a pivotal role. Lazarsfeld and long-time collaborator Robert K. Merton (1956) emphasized the importance of Weberian concepts of social location (class, religion, opportunity structures) over mass mobilization processes in political decision making. The dynamic tensions between personal and public information, on the one hand, and social and political structures on the other, have been profitably investigated by Harold Lasswell (Lasswell, 1935), Hugh Duncan (Duncan, 1962), and Walter Lippmann (Riccio, 1994). These scholars have shown how power and leadership influence what comes to be considered knowledge. At the outset, whenever unframed information is encountered, any number of perspectives may emerge from a vast range of possibilities. These authors show that as the information is processed, only a small set of frames will be used.

From a quite different (and highly technical) tack, Bell Labs mathematician Claude Shannon characterized information as being measured in bits and probabilities. He defined information theory as the problem of "reproducing at one point either exactly or approximately a message selected at another point" (Shannon, 1963: p. 3). Information therefore reduces uncertainty, and the more uncertainty that is removed, the more information any signal or piece of data contains. Shannon helped spawn several domains of inquiry, including theories of encryption and data transmission, and also showed how a variety of technical factors (such as bandwidth, reliability, channel numbers, and signal-to-noise ratios) limited certain system functionalities.

An essential part of Shannon's analysis was the concept of entropy in communication systems. He demonstrates the amount of information that can be transmitted varies directly with the uncertainty that exists in a communication channel. (However, he was careful to say that his use of the word information was not the same as the common usage of the word information, which has the sense of meaningful information.) Shannon's work has proven invaluable in information theory for helping determine optimal technical designs for communication technology systems under various practical scenarios. His ideas influenced control theory, which emphasizes coding, sender, receiver, noise, and feedback. Yet Shannon is far more cited than understood in the social sciences, and his definition of information is too technical to be of substantial interest to the communication scholar. Yet his parsimonious notions, so elegantly proven in mathematical terms, have some intriguing implications for the social sciences, a point returned to at this chapter's conclusion.

Structure and Process

Turning to the social structural and process levels, it may be seen that information (the term used here in its traditional sense of having meaning) is also linked to the notion of change—in theory and practice. Information alters lived reality. Information works to reduce uncertainty and thereby increases control over environments, both natural and social. On a macro level, Manuel Castells (1989) links information processing to culture, seeing it as symbolic manipulation. Information technologies are the systems, devices, and techniques that produce and augment relationships among culture, productive forces, and scientific and other knowledge, They of course operate within a specific sociological and historical cultural setting.

Fritz Machlup's (1962) classic treatment distinguishes between transmission (information) and understanding (knowledge), yet his traditional distinction has come under siege by adherents of the cultural studies movement who see knowledge as power—power wielded not by Plato's benign philosopher king but by exploitative political-economic interests. These interests are often exercised along the lines of militarism, capitalism, gender, and social class and are exploited along the lines of decomposition (Horowitz, 1994) and statism. Mark Poster (1990) holds that "information has become a privileged term in our culture ... and society is divided between the information rich and the information poor." In a related vein, Jean-François Lyotard asserts in *The Postmodern Condition: A Report on Knowledge* (1979 [1984]) that information is not simply scientific knowledge but also encompasses narrative knowledge.

Although Nilsson (1990) links information to change on the level of either real-life practice or thought patterns, it is because information is affecting processes within the human mind. Manuel Castells highlights the cultural dimension of information in *The Informational City: Information Technology, Economic Restructuring, and the Urban-Regional Process* (1989). In this volume, he argues that information is intrinsically linked to culture because information processing is actually the symbolic manipulation of existing knowledge.

Communication theorists deal with information as a conceptual category that, like other forms of discourse and nonverbal communication, can convey meaning. In addition, information has a directional utility, that is, it can be communicated. Nilsson (1990) defines the goal of electronic and communication systems as providing quality information, or, useful information "in a given problem area for a given subject and all effects on any subject and/or object." As with the sociocultural definitions, information is again held to be a social factor that expresses a particular worldview and has discernible effects on social actors.

If knowledge is to serve as an intermediary in contemporary society, then the information that it interprets must be transferable. James Boyle notes (1996) that the easy conversion from one form into another is a central marker of an information society. Ironically, though, Boyle says that as information expands to include "anything," it is commodified to restrict its dissemination and manipulation. While digitalization in theory allows for infinite copies that are identical to the original, copyright laws and technical enhancements can restrict and possibly prevent such copying, and what one has a right, ability, and permission to do continue to be tested.

The two opposing views concerning the ability to copy and reuse information are drawn from a similar inspiration—that society should be regulated to advance the interests of society as a whole and that intellectual property laws should return the greatest good possible to society. Thus the length of time that a copyright restriction may be in force is checked, and some fair use is allowed even of copyrighted material. As an inducement for investing effort to create valuable intellectual property, however, those who create the works are rewarded for their efforts and control the copying and use of their creations.

From a social-relativistic view, justice demands that those who are least able to pay for materials ought to be able to have fair use those materials. Advocates of this viewpoint often argue that the poor would not have bought the intellectual property anyway or that another digital copy can be made cost-free. These arguments are often used by students or by people in less-developed countries to justify making copies of software. Advocates of copyright-free approaches also hold that worthwhile intellectual property should be created for its own sake and that society benefits by not having barriers to information.

This argument for copyright-free reproduction is countered by the view that creators of works should be the ones who decide who gets to use them and how. Without incentives, the necessary efforts (and investments) would not be made that allow information to be brought forth to the public. In the area of computer operating-system software, one company (Xerox) created approaches that another company (Microsoft) later reengineered and used, leading to the birth of one of the world's largest commercial empires. But at the same time, open systems that are based on freeware (Linux) have been used on a no-cost basis and a proprietary basis (Red Hat). This area will undoubtedly continue to be contested since, if one can put it too simply, the formal rule-making bodies tend to support property claims while innovators and users in the general populace look for ways that information can be free for the taking. Too, leaders of less-developed countries are often highly motivated to seek ways to overturn intellectual property regimes that work to their country's disadvantage. This situation is true of many forms of information, from music to pharmaceutical formulae to book publishing (Horowitz, 1991).

Prediction and Control

For most of human history, technological limitations made moving information from one place to another difficult. Many societies were nonetheless deeply engaged with patterned abstraction in the form of religious practices and beliefs, as the great pyramids ofTeotihuacan and Egypt attest. Institutions of major religions, such as the Catholic Church, have been centrally concerned with detecting patterns and communicating and reinforcing these interpretations. So all in all, there certainly have for centuries been systems for distributing information and gaining feedback on that distribution. Although the technologies used in these processes were highly varied, and included scriptoria, runners, heralds, and signal fires, they were nothing if not cumbersome.

Yet, once the essential problem of reducing information to electrical impulses was solved, information could be transmitted ever more cheaply and widely. This in turn unleashed tremendous advances in the way that information was produced, processed, and consumed, with important economic, political, and social ramifications. Notably, they have enabled information to be moved more easily (that is, communicated), which has allowed the creation of markets to supply the information and the means for its transmission. By strategically controlling the creation, transmission, and application of information, enormous commercial empires in information distribution developed in the fields of telegraphy, telephony, newspapers, television, and radio. Secondary markets quickly developed to use information to adjust for risk; today these take the forms that include stock markets and the insurance industry. Tertiary markets also opened to gather and apply information in the institutions of scientific research, higher education, financial accounting, and consultancies. These yielded quaternary markets—including the by-products of transactions (such as frequent-flyer programs) and location information (such as mobile telephone monitoring systems)—that can be useful for applications including marketing and law enforcement.

A most important question concerning social equity in the information society involves the "digital divide"—the division between those with and without access to digital data. This is because information is seen as the essential ingredient to effective and comfortable living. Increasingly, the utility of information and thus the quality of its meaning are coming to be measured in its price. At the same time, there is continuing policy pressure to adjust marketplace dynamics in light of concerns over differential access to information and to what extent information equity across demographic groupings should be a target of action by governmental or international bodies.

Many critics see a progression in the pivotal function of knowledge and predict its increasing commodification. This in turn may lead to information possessors ignoring its "use-value" and treating it as an end in itself, to be used when profits may be expected.

Lyotard (1984 [1979]) even claims that learning will circulate as money. In a parallel vein, Lessig (2001) and others assert that technology does not directly lead to the production of original knowledge but creates more paths and links between information—such as linked webpages or Wikipedia functions online—which themselves become a vital source of new knowledge.

It is possible that the personal, mediated communication typical of the Internet, especially when it is further enhanced with mobile applications, will be a qualitative change of a magnitude that equals the change from the industrial era to the information society. In this regard, Irwin Lebow (1995) holds that the phrase "information superhighway" confuses "information" with "communication": networked information access actually includes communication and entertainment, and from the user's viewpoint these applications are often the central attractions.

Information Society

The following section highlights some major theoretical perspectives on the social role of information. Of course, the various perspectives may be classified in a number of different ways. One general way is to look at information within the context of its ambient society. Alistair S. Duff in *Information Society Studies* (2000), for instance, examines the information sector, the information explosion, and the information technology diffusion, which contribute to his methodology for finding valid grounds for the phenomenon of the information society. Another general way is to focus on information in a societal setting, that is, in the "Information Society." As an example, Frank Webster (1994) isolates five analytical approaches to defining the information society: technological, means of economic production, occupational structure, spatial array, and cultural definitions.

In a blended approach, the classification categories below can also be used to suggest understandings of how information shapes and is shaped by social forces.

The economic approach, as its name denotes, defines information and the society in which it exists through a lens that emphasizes production, market, and consumption aspects. Researchers pursuing this direction highlight the rapid expansion of the number of people who work in the information sector of the economy. Fritz

Machlup (1962) introduced this approach with his study of national data, where he defines *knowledge* as a state of knowing that "is produced by activities such as talking plus listening, writing plus reading, but also by activities such as discovering, inventing, intuiting." Knowledge producers transmit or communicate information, receive and process information, invest knowledge, and create instruments for the production of knowledge (such as typewriters, copy machines, and computers). As a result, according to Machlup, the information industry is composed chiefly of workers in the educational sphere, other white-collar industry workers who participate in managerial tasks, and some blue-collar workers (such as pressmen, lithographers, and typesetters). Machlup's seminal 1962 contributions have yet to be superseded. Nonetheless, there are many notable attempts to measure the information outputs of societies and compare international knowledge flows. A related intellectual development has been to measure the information produced by scientific communities and develop indexes of scientific productivity. Derek deSolla Price (1965) was an early pioneer of this approach. Price documented the exponential rise of scientific publications and knowledge across the globe and across several centuries. He dubbed his approach "scientometrics," and his path has been developed by scholars who have applied social network analysis to the process, with fertile results.

Many advocates of the idea of socioeconomic transformation through information have been attracted to the idea of the "postindustrial society." Two of this position's most widely recognized proponents, Alain Touraine and Daniel Bell, have been influenced by Marxist interpretations of class movement and hold that in the postindustrial society the production and processing of information are core activities that are engaged in at all levels of production, distribution, consumption, and management. Touraine's "programmed society" is structured by its production methods and economic organization. He claims that the present social conflict is between economic and political decision making, that this new society is "technocratic" (as defined by the nature of its ruling class), and that the working class is no longer a unified political agent. Similarly, Bell predicts in his *The Coming of Post-Industrial Society* (1973) a shift of labor away from goods-producing industries and toward white-collar service and information-producing industries as well as moves in society toward sexual equality and communal consciousness. Bell identifies a "knowledge class" that derives its power from a dual axis of technology and knowledge. While Bell takes a more economic approach and Touraine writes through a sociopolitical lens, both theorists see the sociologist as having a privileged place as a "seer" of sorts who can understand and direct the postindustrial society. In this sense, they take a page from Auguste Comte who saw society guided by sociologist-priests.

For Bell, scientific knowledge and values will be involved in the political process in the postindustrial society, and intellectual work will be bureaucratized. While he calls this new society "postindustrial" rather than "knowledge-based" or "informational," clearly one source of power in it is possession or ownership of knowledge. Jacques Ellul in *The Technological Society* (1954 [1964]) also posits the coming society as a technological society—not entirely based on technology but rather using carefully planned "techniques" to achieve its goals.

Marc Porat and Michael Rubin in *The Information Economy: Development and Measurement* (1977) also see the transition of the labor force from manual to informational work as the foundation of the informational society. Following closely after Ellul and Bell, Porat identifies two information sectors—the major information goods and services producers (industries that produce, process, or distribute information) and the secondary public and private bureaucracies (organizations that engage in research, development, record keeping, and governmental planning). Like Machlup and Bell, Porat uses economic data to support his claims.

While most theorists agree in principle that trends in the way information affects social and economic organization can be identified and assessed, they have different opinions about the social effects of these trends. For liberals such as Lord Ralf Dahrendorf (1975), economic growth and social change are necessary prerequisites to social improvement and require a free flow of information. For Marxists, such as Herb Schiller (1984), however, information is associated with advanced capitalism in crisis. His three themes are that market criteria and pressures are important in creating new information; that class inequalities figure prominently in the distribution of, access to, and generation of information; and that social organization is dominated by corporate capitalism. For Libertarian and conservative advocates such as Peter Huber (1997), the information society has unbounded potential for raising standards of living, increasing comfort, and sparking creativity, if only the hamstringing efforts of governmental entities would get out of the way and cease imposing their collectivist values on others. Those theorists who see the information society as radically different from past societies are inclined to be optimistic about its possibilities, whereas those who see the information society as a progression from past societies tend to predict a downward spiral. In a sense, this is a twenty-first century continuation of a battle whose lines were clearly drawn during the nineteenth century. Materialists (such as Karl Marx) profoundly disagreed with idealists (such as Max Weber), and this conflict continues today, extending to the social role of information. Materialists tend to see information as a means of production, existing within the social structure. Idealists see information as gaining an existence independent of particular social circumstances.

Strategic Information

Turning to another area of debate, the political regulation-school approach to examining the information society is similar to the economic approach but is linked to political processes. Regulation-school theorists, such as Michel Aglietta in *A Theory of Capitalist Regulation: The U.S. Experience* (1979) and Alain Lipietz in *Mirages and Miracles: The Crises of Global Fordism* (1987), examine the mode of accumulation in a given society and the relationship of accumulation to its mode of regulation. According to Lipietz, after a period characterized by the mass consumption of goods by blue-collar workers, the mass consumption of goods, nation-state oligopolies, there now exists a post-Fordist era. This post-Fordist period has witnessed the disintegration of vertical organization, a strategy of outsourcing, an international division of labor, and an assault on organized labor as a whole. The post-Fordist period is also marked by substantial flexibility in production, consumption, and employment. When mass production declines, the individual emerges as much more individualistic and consumption-centered, and information takes on an individualistic representation as people find their own information and even become information producers on their own.

There are, of course, many other approaches to regulation. One of them is the regulation-analytic school, which focuses on influences on policymakers and the values that come into play. In this vein, Gerald Brock in *Telecommunication Policy for the Information Age: From Monopoly to Competition* (1998) examines what he calls a theory of decentralized public decision-making. According to Brock, this model generates rational outcomes consistent with public preferences.

By contrast, neo-Marxist Dan Schiller in *Digital Capitalism: Networking the Global Market System* (1999), as well as theorists across the political spectrum, fears the convergence of control over all information media in a few large multinational corporations. The nature of public life, the autonomy of consumers, and the quality of education would be the big losers. Schiller holds that cyberspace will be the handmaiden of this unprecedented centralization of power, which will advance consumerism on a transnational scale, particularly among privileged groups in various countries. Interestingly, there are always new anecdotes that support both the regulation-analytic and monopoly capitalism viewpoints. Evidence for one viewpoint may be seen in the buying up of small firms and concentration of market power by Microsoft, Yahoo, and Google, as well as in the proliferation of intellectual property strictures by governmental regimes. These instances would seem to support the monopoly capitalism viewpoint. On the other hand, the proliferation of new firms, exciting and novel services and creation of new challengers to old entrenched players offer support for the liberal viewpoint. Even as Google buys up new companies, it is challenging entrenched stalwarts such as Microsoft, even as Microsoft supplanted IBM in market dominance. Despite conflicting claims, it does appear that over the long run the company that dominates the information industry in one period cannot transition to a new era. This may be illustrated by Western Union, a telegraph company, which declined to buy the patent for the telephone, supposedly deprecating the invention as a "mere toy." Western Union was bought up by the telephone company AT&T. AT&T as an organization was unable to survive the transition to the digital-Internet world. Indeed, even Google itself seems to prove the point that the best approach is not necessarily to own the information but rather to control the roadmap to the information.

Turning from the economic and macro-social aspects of information, attention can be usefully devoted to the political side of information creation and use. In this domain, several theorists see information as intrinsic to political processes and even the nation-state as a whole. Jürgen Habermas in *The Structural Transformation of the Public Sphere: An Inquiry into a Category of Bourgeois Society* (1962 [1992]) builds a theory that information is the center of the public sphere, which is the hub of information *qua* social knowledge. In this view, information underpins all the processes of a democratic society, and is the sine qua non. The public sphere is the source discourse, it functions to construct knowledge, especially political knowledge, out of the information input of its members.

Information is a fundamental element of economic organization, political processes, public spheres, and nation-states. As it always has, it also continues to play a large role in defining the military realm. Webster (1994) points out the increasing predominance of information warfare that uses intelligence and informational technologies on the battlefield. This is not simply a metaphor. Rather, information, as has always been the case, is critical to military success. Keegan (2004) argues that while traditional intelligence is critical in both traditional warfare and anti-terror operations, it can become the decisive factor in terms of the latter. He also outlines the difficulty of effective information evaluation when applied to covert organizations. He is one of the many skeptics concerning the effectiveness information collection and use when a centralized organization, such as the U.S. Department of Defense, attempts to fight a network and decentralized organization, such as al-Qaida.

Global Systems

On a still grander scale, Manuel Castells uses a world-systems perspective to explore the recent historical transition from development by capitalism to development by information (Castells, 2001). He posits a strong link between knowledge and economic growth, showing that the heretofore intermediate stage of technological development is unnecessary. Instead, he holds that knowledge can perform the technological function of producing informatization—knowledge alone may be the basis of production in the informational society. How is this new development to take place? According to Castells, information is both the raw material and the outcome of technological change. Information-processing activities in the industrial mode of development were fostered by two major factors—the central organizational capacities of the large corporation and the shift in the sources of productivity from capital and labor to factors such as science and technology. Information-consumption activities were fostered by two additional factors—the need for information gathering and distributing flows to connect between buyer and seller in the mass-market environment and the state's role in assuming collective management of goods and services. The state, in turn, establishes information systems that set the codes and rules that govern citizens' lives.

Another global information theorist is Robert Reich (1991). He echoes Bell by highlighting the rise of the job category of advanced information processing, which he dubs "symbolic-analytic services." These services are not involved in the trading of tangible objects but rather in the manipulation of symbols and visual representations. Workers are problem solvers in that "they simplify reality into abstract images that can be rearranged, juggled, experimented with, communicated to other specialists, and then, eventually, transformed back into reality" (Reich, 1991: p. 177). Whereas "professionals" of the earlier regime attained mastery of a particular knowledge domain, symbolic-analysts work by using, not learning, knowledge. They draw on established bodies of knowledge to rearrange and analyze information that already exists. In this way, the symbolic-analyst is changing the nature of information from static and isolated to dynamic and integrated. Additionally, the rise of the symbolic-analyst leads to a breakdown in traditional hierarchies of information provision. Workers rise in the job market not because of hard work or technical expertise but because of inventiveness and creativity: "the only true competitive advantage lies in skill in solving, identifying, and brokering new problems." For these theorists, the widespread availability of information, and not technology itself, has far-reaching social implications. Perhaps one of the most striking is the way that ideas can flow easily across borders, even while people cannot, which will impact the international economic order and spill over into the quality of lives for millions in both developed and developing nations.

One common framework for interpreting the information society is technological innovation, especially in telecommunications. "Information technology (IT) diffusion" can be measured by the scope of the IT revolution and the proliferation of computer technology (Duff, 2000). Frederick Williams remarks that the information society "is a society where the economy reflects growth owing to technological advances." Michael J. Piore and Charles F. Sabel use the term "flexible specialization" to refer to independent, small businesses that analyze and respond to markets far more efficiently than large corporations can.

Simon Nora and Alain Minc in *The Computerization of Society: A Report to the President of France* (1980) were the first to propose the term "informatization" to represent the union of computers, telecommunication systems, and social organizations that lead to a greater informational society. Their report presented knowledge as the "engine of growth" and warned of the dangers of non-informational paths of development. Herbert S. Dordick and Georgette Wang in *The Information Society: A Retrospective View* (1993: p. 60) enlarge this interpretation to define "informatization" along three dimensions—infrastructural, economic, and social. Informatization, therefore, may be measured by the number of telephone lines, newspapers, computers, and television sets in a society, as well as the number of workers who are engaged in information technology and the size of the information sector's contribution to a nation's gross domestic product. With the Internet's rapid growth, these aspects can only be part of the picture. Access to the Internet, and the number of people and amount of time involved with web activities, including weblogs or blogs, must be considered. Yet even as the technology changes, the basic principles seem to remain as pertinent in the twenty-first century as they were a half-century before.

Cultural Systems

Cultural studies, which developed strongly since the 1980s, has also had much to contribute to understanding the subtler aspects of the rising of the information society. This view contrasts with economic orientations towards the information society, which emphasize the technological-drivers, and treats qualities of the information society as objective, measurable entities. A cultural studies approach sees society as a dynamic and multilayered process, and so not open to definitive measurement or instrumentation; more precisely, they see measurement and instrumentation as methodologically misleading and irrelevant. For instance, cultural theorist Jean

Baudrillard (1983) views information as being produced equally by all people and as having no singular meaning or interpretation. Information can thus be interpreted as essentially meaningless. However, he sees that people impose their meanings on information, and the resulting structure as largely arbitrary. Another meta-framing, as Ron Day shows in *The Modern Invention of Information* (2001), is that there have been many information ages, and that the concept itself divorces power from its historical context. Day notes the real history is a troubled one of winners and losers. Thus, to Day, cultural studies can retrieve the banished history of information's construction and application so that the deeper experiences can be appreciated.

The cultural studies approach stands in stark contrast to the possibly teleological and certainly evolutionary/progressive models of Price and Bell. The approaches part ways on many questions, including the usefulness of detailed quantitative analysis. Cultural studies, while often rich and provocative, benefits by being complemented by its erstwhile rival of empiricism. The intellectual processes of discernment, categorization, and testing of empirical data are vital to the firmer understanding of social processes. Without counterbalancing, the ideas of post-modernists may themselves become a sealed domain of competing sets of rhetoric, disconnected from the very processes they purport to describe.

Social and Political Forms

The long-term implications of the increasing use of digital communication has also attracted the interest of social critics. This is partly because cheap, digital information when combined with networked computers has led directly to new social forms and interaction patterns. Some predict negative consequences for social interaction from these changes. Sherry Turkle in *Life on the Screen: Identity in the Age of the Internet* (1995) sees a wilderness of mirrors in which a new identity is produced through online interactions, an identity which can only be considered synthetic. As a result, senses of community and integration are lost as people flee unpleasant "real-world" social situations for a "life on the screen," that is, for online pretending and role experimentation.

James E. Katz and Ronald E. Rice, in *Social Consequences of Internet Use* (2002), offer a brighter picture in their study of involvement with groups and communities through the Internet (social capital), and use of the Internet for social interaction and expression (identity). Their conclusions are based on surveys of Internet users and non-users that include the earliest comparative public-opinion surveys about the Internet as well as cross-national comparisons between the United States and the United Kingdom. They also examine Internet use in various countries. Katz and Rice conclude that the Internet far from reducing social capital actually contributes to it. Perhaps less controversially, they also find that the Internet enables novel forms of social interaction and self-expression. One such novel form of information they discuss is the weblog, or blog phenomenon. These are a novel blending of diary and self-expression that erase the lines of public and private spheres. While blogs have been decried as a "wasteland of self-important nobodies" (Anon, 2004), Katz and Rice hold that they provide a valuable opportunity for people to express themselves and create new relationships. While Katz and Rice agree that misuse can occur with any information system, including the Internet, they conclude that the Internet fosters opportunities for satisfying individual interests while providing collective benefits to society.

Incisive social critic and sociologist, C. Wright Mills, anticipated many of the arguments presented above. He held that "knowledge is no longer widely felt as an ideal; it is seen as an instrument. In a society of power and wealth, knowledge is valued as an instrument of power and wealth." He went on to identify numerous ways in which this proposition was supported, most famously in *The Power Elite* (1956).

The ancient view that knowledge is power was also picked up by Michel Foucault in *Discipline and Punish: The Birth of the Prison* (1975 [1979]). There he advanced provocative ideas about information in a social context and why information (and resulting knowledge) is such a coveted commodity. According to him, knowledge is synonymous with power. He presents the Panopticon, a prison in which guards can see into every cell but prisoners see neither guards nor other prisoners. The guards therefore have the advantage of knowledge over the prisoners' activities. As the prisoners internalize the idea that they are constantly under surveillance, they begin to self-regulate, and thus the guards have attained power over their inmates. However, if a prisoner learns that he is not being watched, he may try to escape; the prisoner attains power over the guard as a result of this knowledge. For Foucault, the relationship between power and knowledge is inseparable, so that knowledge always grows out of power relations and vice versa. In the context of the information society, a reading of Foucault may sensitize us to the inherent power relations that underlie flows of information and the effects that information and social knowledge can have on social order and form.

While Foucault takes a highly theoretical approach to power and society, Bell draws a more concrete relation between knowledge holders and the ruling class. For Bell, the codification of knowledge, especially in the technical and scientific professions, plays an increasingly important role in maintaining society. As a result, a highly trained and intellectualized elite will lead further social progress.

On the other hand, Boyle (1996) maintains that the information society may actually lead to horizontal social progress and that the *idea* of information has become so fluid and pervasive as to completely dissolve disciplinary boundaries. For example, gene mapping as a topic has spread from biological discourse to pervade discussions by social scientists, engineers, and artists. At the same time, information has become a value-added dimension of commercial products that needs to be protected. As technological materials (such as digital storage media) become cheaper, their informational or intellectual content makes up a greater part of the end product's value.

This shift is echoed by Lyotard, who believes that knowledge is increasingly becoming an informational commodity. Because knowledge as a commodity is vital to maintaining productive power, nation-states may "fight for the control of information, just as they battled in the past for control over territory, and afterwards for control of access to and exploitation of raw materials and cheap labor." The state no longer has a monopoly on the distribution of knowledge and information. As the need for transparent and clear information begins to underpin society, economic interests butt heads with the state, and the state grows powerless to control information and knowledge dissemination and must reexamine its traditional role in guiding technological progress.

For the optimists of the information society, notably Yoneji Masuda (1981), information access encourages people to participate in democracy and to improve the environment by working from home and spending more time in creative, intellectual work.

For him and other optimists, informatization can redress and prevent social problems like the unequal distribution of wealth and slow economic development. Melvin Kranzberg (1985) likewise believes that the increased production of knowledge in the information society will allow people to understand better their options and the consequences of their actions, thus preventing catastrophic wars. Even earlier, the theorist Kenneth E. Boulding (1964) proposed the term "post-civilization" to describe the freedom that he expected the information society to bring out of the Marxist socioeconomic class revolutions of the past. According to Boulding, as the information society builds up the sphere of the self-conscious social against the individual, general mental evolution will guide further social progression.

Near Futures

Wireless mobile communication promises to be the next information revolution as it changes people's work and study habits and their activities in public space (Katz, 2003). When mobile communication is combined with the Internet, new problems arise, but so do novel social and economic opportunities that are comparable to those precipitated by the computer and that can enrich the lives of vast numbers of people from all backgrounds and all regions of the world.

For many centuries, various experts thought that increased information would yield better lives, and that enhanced communication would lead to harmonious social interaction, perhaps even an end to strife and war. In terms of material lives, improved technology based on better information has eased many material burdens so that an ordinary worker in industrial society typically has a life of comfort (air conditioning, antibiotics, television) that was beyond the reach of the richest mogul. In terms of the second contention, it may be that the opposite is true. While a faster flow of information can lead to enhanced lives on the material level, it can also speed the flow of wrong, misleading, or scary information. It is possible that a corollary obtains, namely that new information technologies, such as the mobile phone, can give rise to anxiety: one must be in touch and ready to react. Or that making more information available, such as is the case with Internet websites and blogs, can keep alive, and even stimulate the growth of dissident political movements and attacks on even the largest media empires.

Moreover, information flows can lead to demands for transparency and accountability at every level from institutional to microsocial. So instead of being a fountainhead of freedom, increased information can lead to demands for increased constraints and monitoring. From a sociological perspective, there are many ironies of information flow.

It is worth noting too that much attention has been paid to sociological analyses of information that emphasize potential monopolistic and exploitative practices of the owners of media content. Yet the Marxist-inspired view that the centralized control of the means of production, in this case of information, determines material conditions is being turned on its head due to technological advances. This line of argument was pioneered by Ithiel de Sola Pool, who declared that technologies of freedom aim at pluralism of expression rather than a dissemination of prefabricated ideas (Pool, 1983). Pool's prescient ideas have become realized—perhaps more profoundly than even he might have imagined—as communication became the catalysts that broke up the Soviet Empire and the ousting of authoritarians from the Ukraine to Georgia to the Philippines. The novel and ever-increasing array of alternative communication systems continues to surprise and amaze social scientists. These range from Internet steganography and web cams to mobile phone videos, alterative reality games and geo-positional monitoring. These proliferating and ingenious applications have severely eroded dominant paradigms of elites and the power of traditional monopolistic "one-to-many" technologies (such as newspaper publishing, broadcast television, and major film studios).

Because of personal communication technology, information has lost its absolute centrality as part of a Marxist superstructure of production that sits atop society. It has instead become a form of struggle within society and its growing number of co-producers. Despite unceasing efforts to the contrary at the level of policymaking, information is becoming ever more fungible as a commodity even while its meaning and interpretation becomes more contested. More voices are raised in every quarter, and there is an open contest over knowledge claims. Even while more data is collected at the level of the individual social actor, dictators around the world are confronted by information they would wish to banish. But the invariant principles demonstrated by Shannon have an unexpected human impact. It seems clear that the more competing explanations one has for any phenomena, the less certainty one has in any particular explanation. Information can be helpful up to a point, but when there is always more information out there, always more information coming, decisions can become harder not easier.

The ultimate irony, then, may be that while the narrow definition of information discussed at the chapter's outset—that information is uncertainty reduction—is germane at local levels, the larger impact may be the opposite: knowledge leads to growth in uncertainty and psychological tension. Shannon's axioms, as it turns out, are extremely apposite to social science and public policy: increased information also leads to increased uncertainty. It does this in the soft terms of human lives lived every bit as much as in the hard terms of communication network efficiencies achieved.

References

Aglietta, M. (1979). *A theory of capitalist regulation: The U.S. experience*. London: New Left Books.

Anon. (2004). *Wall Street Journal Online,* March 16. Retrieved from http://online.wsj.com/public/us.

Baudrillard, Jean (1983). *In the shadow of the silent majorities*. (Paul Foss, John Johnston, and Paul Patton, Trans.). New York: Semiotext(e).

Bell, Daniel (1973). *The coming of post-industrial society: A venture in social forecasting*. New York: Basic Books.

Boulding, Kenneth (1964). *The meaning of the twentieth century: The great transition*. New York: HarperCollins.

Boyle, James (1996). *Shamans, software, and spleens: Law and the construction of the information society*. Cambridge, MA: Harvard University Press.

Brock, G. (1998). *Telecommunication policy for the information age: From monopoly to competition*. Cambridge, MA: Harvard University Press.

Castells, Manuel (1989). *The informational city: Information technology, economic restructuring, and the urban-regional process*. Oxford: Blackwell.

Castells, Manuel (2000). *The Internet Galaxy*. New York: Oxford University Press.

Dahrendorf, Ralf (1975). *The new liberty: Survival and justice in a changing world*. Stanford, CA: Stanford University Press.

Day, Ron (2001). *The modern invention of information: Discourse, history, and power*. Carbondale: Southern Illinois University Press.

Dordick, Herbert S., and G. Wang. (1993). *The information society: A retrospective view*. Newbury Park, CA: Sage.

Duff, Alistair (2000). *Information society studies*. London: Routledge.

Duncan, Hugh D. (1962). *Communication and social order*. Oxford University Press, New York.

Ellul, Jacques (1964 [1954]). *The technological society*. New York: Vintage Books.

Foucault, Michel (1979). *Discipline and punish: The birth of the prison* (A. Sheridan, Trans.). New York: Vintage Books.

Goddard, J. (1992). Networks of transactions. In K. Robins (Ed.), *Understanding information: Business, technology and geography)*. London: Belhaven Press, pp. 178-201.

Habermas, Jürgen (1992 [1962]). *The structural transformation of the public sphere: An inquiry into a category of bourgeois society* (T. Burger and F. Lawrence, Trans). Cambridge: Polity Press.

Horowitz, Irving L. (1991). *Communicating ideas: The politics of scholarly publishing.* New Brunswick: Transaction Publishers.

Horowitz, Irving L. (1994). *The decomposition of sociology.* New York: Oxford University Press.

Huber, Peter W. (1997). *Law and disorder in cyberspace.* New York: Oxford University Press.

IBM Community Development Foundation. (1997). *The net result: Social inclusion in the information society—Report of the [U.K.] National Working Party on social inclusion.* London: IBM U.K.

Katz, James E. (2003). A nation of ghosts? Choreography of mobile communication in public spaces. In Kristof Nyiri (Ed.), *Mobile democracy: Essays on society, self and politics.* Vienna: Passagen Verlag, pp. 21-32.

Katz, James E., and Ronald E. Rice (2002). *Social consequences of Internet use: Access, involvement, and interaction.* Cambridge, MA: MIT Press.

Keegan, John (2004). *Intelligence in war: The value—and limitations—of what the military can learn about the enemy.* New York: Vintage.

Kranzberg, Melvin (1985). The information age: Evolution or revolution? In B. R. Guild (Ed.), *Information technologies and social transformation.* Washington, DC: National Academy Press, pp. 35-53.

Lasswell, Harold D. (1935). *World politics and personal insecurity.* New York: Whittlesey House, McGraw-Hill.

Lazarsfeld, Paul, Bernard Berelson and Hazel Gaudet (1944). *The people's choice.* New York: Duell, Sloan and Pearce.

Lebow, Irwin (1995). *Information highways and byways: From the telegraph to the twenty-first century.* New York: Wiley/Institute of Electrical and Electronics Engineers Press.

Lessig, Lawrence (2001). *The nature of ideas: The fate of the commons in a connected world.* New York: Random House.

Lipietz, Alain (1993), *Fordism and post-Fordism.* In W. Outhwaite and Tom Bottomore, *The Blackwell Dictionary of Twentieth Century Social Thought*, Oxford: Blackwell's, pp. 230-231.

Lipietz, Alain (1987). *Mirages and miracles: The crises of global Fordism.* London: Verso.

Lyotard, Jean-Francois (1984 [1979]). *The postmodern condition: A report on knowledge* (G. Bennington and B. Massumi, Trans.). Manchester: Manchester University Press.

Machlup, Fritz (1962). *The production and distribution of knowledge in the United States.* Princeton, NJ: Princeton University Press.

Masuda, Yoneji (1981). *The information society as post-industrial society.* Washington, DC: World Future Society.

Merton, Robert K. (1968). *Social theory and social structure.* (Second revised edition.) New York: Free Press.

Mills, C. Wright (1956). *The power elite.* New York: Oxford University Press.

Nilsson, P. (1990). The distortion of information. In J. Berleur, A. Clement, R. Sizer, and D. Whitehouse (Eds.), *The information society: Evolving landscapes.* New York: Springer-Verlag, pp. 449-459.

Nora, Simon and Alain Minc (1980). *The computerization of society: A report to the president of France.* Cambridge, MA: MIT Press.

Piore, Michael and Charles Sabel (1984). *The second industrial divide: Possibilities for prosperity.* New York: Basic Books.

Pool, Ithiel de Sola (1983). *Technologies of freedom.* Cambridge, MA: Harvard Belknap Press.

Porat, Marc U. and Michael Rubin (1977). *The information economy: Development and measurement.* Washington, DC: U.S. Government Printing Office.

Porat, Marc U. (1978). Communication policy in an information society. In G. O. Robinson (Ed.), *Communications for tomorrow: Policy perspectives for the 1980s.* New York: Praeger, pp. 3-60.

Poster, Mark (1990). *The mode of information: Poststructuralism and social context.* Cambridge: Polity Press.

Price, Derek deSolla (1963). *Little science, big science.* New York: Columbia University Press.

Reich, Robert B. (1991). *The work of nations: Preparing ourselves for twenty-first-century capitalism.* New York: Vintage.

Riccio, Barry D. (1994). *Walter Lippmann—Odyssey of a liberal.* New Brunswick, NJ: Transaction Publishers.

Schiller, Daniel (1999). *Digital capitalism: Networking the global market system.* Cambridge, MA: MIT Press.

Schiller, Herbert I. (1984). *Information and the crisis economy.* Norwood, NJ: Ablex.

Shannon, Claude E. (1963 [1948]). The Mathematical Theory of Communication . In Claude E. Shannon and Warren Weaver, *The Mathematical Theory of Communication.* Champaign: U. Illinois Press, pp. 3-6.

Touraine, Alain (1971 [1969]). *The post-industrial society: Tomorrow's social history—Classes, conflicts and culture in the programmed society* (Leonard F. X. Mayhew, Trans.). New York: Random House.

Turkle, Sherry (1995). *Life on the screen: Identity in the age of the Internet.* New York: Simon and Schuster.

Webster, Frank (1994). What information society? *Information Society 10*(1): 1-24.

Williams, Fred (Ed.). (1988). *Measuring the information society: The Texas studies.* London: Sage.

10

Future Communication Technology and Social Settings: A Speculative Exercise

Speculating about the future can be intriguing. It can also be useful because doing so can help us understand and appreciate what exists, and where changes may be forthcoming, and perhaps later let us know how far off the mark we were in our guesses. This is all the more the case when we think about the communication systems that surround people, and how these may be changing in the decades ahead. How will life be lived in the year 2076, two hundred years after the telephone's invention? What for example will computers, monitoring systems and robots in the coming years be able to know about us, do for us, and to us?

Future speculations often fall into a groove of a persistent interest more in the machines that could be developed than the social relationships that could emerge from the technology. Not that the latter have been ignored, but rather there has been a much stronger emphasis on machinery. One can see this consistency in discourses about the future if one compares Sir Francis Bacon's ruminations in the *Novum Organum,* published in 1620 to today's blogs.

The gap can be striking between writers asking questions about biology and technology versus the way that advances in science and technology might affect our social relationships and even our inner selves—our seemingly human nature. This is nowhere more true than in the area of communication. How will the "machinery" with which we now spend our time, and also use for passing information to each other (and keep for later use), be changed and with what consequences? Moreover, what parts of our lives will likely be left relatively untouched by advances in communication technology?

Humans versus Machines: Intellectual Legacies

Although it is an oversimplification, commentators on the future of technology and society generally can be seen as falling into one of two broad groups: utopians or dystopians. When the topic is the machines of the future, both groups see machines supplanting humans in the performance of certain activities.. Where they differ is on the human condition afterward. Utopians often anticipate that humans will be enjoying superlative service rendered by helpful machines; dystopians, that machines will be enjoying sullen service rendered by helpless humans.

Both traditions of futurism have long and honorable histories, but their emphases are quite different. Utopian speculation stresses those areas in which the quality of life will be most improved—physical comfort, material abundance, and social harmony. The American writer Edward Bellamy's *Looking Backward, 2000-1887* (1951 [1888]) and the American behavioral psychologist B.F. Skinner's *Walden Two* (1948) are milestones in this tradition. Dystopian speculation, on the other hand, tends to focus on three interrelated areas in which humanity will suffer the most: individual privacy, personal autonomy, and peace of mind.

The epitome of the pessimistic view is the British novelist George Orwell's *Nineteen Eighty-Four*, (1949) which describes a future in which all personal communication and activity is constantly spied upon by a variety of human and electronic agents and in which any deviation from mindless conformity is punished severely. Technology plays an important part in the effectuation of dystopias, and in some visions it is the machines themselves that are responsible for the downturn of events. An early treatment of the idea of a takeover by our creations is the Czech writer Karel Čapek's dramatic play *R.U.R.: Rossum's Universal Robots* (1920). Its dystopian theme has been a familiar refrain ever since and has received treatment in a variety of media, including many books and films. (A prime example is the 1969 movie *Colossus: The Forbin Project*, about U.S. and Soviet super-computers linking up to rule the world.)

The idea that our technological creations may dehumanize us, if not succeed us altogether, has hit home more forcefully and expressly with the advent of artificial-intelligence research. The American computer scientist Raymond Kurzweil (1999) has predicted that forms of machine intelligence will integrate with us, and then eclipse our old selves, to the extent that "humans who do not utilize such implants are unable to meaningfully participate in dialogues with those who do." Another computer scientist, Hans Moravec (1998) of Carnegie Mellon University, Pittsburgh, Pennsylvania, has commented that sentient, nonbiologically based creatures will far surpass us and, in our stead, colonize the wide-open universe.

Along with these more orchestrated visions have been a variety of casual observations, some of them focusing specifically on how communication devices might be used to interfere with the privacy, peace, and liberty of the ordinary citizen. One writer saw that a certain incipient communication technology would assemble "all mankind upon one great plane, where they can see everything that is done, and hear everything that is said, and judge of every policy that is pursued at the very moment when these events take place" (Quoted in Briggs, 1989).

Although the statement might seem directed to some computer-intensive technology of the twenty-first century, it is, in fact, the British prime minister Lord Salisbury's assessment in the 1880s of the anticipated social impact of the telegraph. Note that the telegraph was expected to have the same destructive effect on privacy that today's critics of the computer predict for the coming decades. It is easy to overestimate as well as underestimate the influence of an emerging communication technology. Even the telegraph's inventor, Samuel Morse, said in 1838 that the telegraph would soon "diffuse with the speed of thought, a knowledge of all that is occurring throughout the land" (Czitrom, 1982). Like the telegraph, the telephone was frequently criticized in its early years for its intrusiveness and disruption of privacy.

In 1895 the *Electrician* magazine ventured that "if a round robin could be got from all quarters we suspect that a majority could be obtained for voting the telephone an unmitigated nuisance which everybody would wish to see abated and perhaps even abolished altogether." In 1913 a writer in *Woman's Home Companion* described the phone as "a noisy intrusion on privacy," complaining about how callers forced themselves on people during meal times, pinning them to the phone "while your dinner turns cold." More modern, but similar complaints have been leveled at telemarketers who draw upon exhaustive research to learn exactly what pitch will most likely keep us pinned on the telephone while our "dinner turns cold" (quoted in Katz, 1999).

One recent communication innovation, the mobile telephone, has been attacked for its disruption of concentration and solitude in places ranging from beaches and movie theaters to restaurants and even houses of worship. Beyond causing inconvenience and embarrassment, mobile phones also have had harmful consequences. Surveys demonstrate that drivers distracted by their mobile phones cause traffic accidents that kill and injure numerous people and account for billions of dollars in damages annually. Despite this toll, both subscribership and usage of mobile phones continue to rise. Speculations about the way that technology will affect life and liberty are thus notable in terms of their consistency, concern, and predisposition.

My own view, specifically concentrating on communication technology, differs from those of Èapek, Kurzweil, and others who see our machines enslaving or dehumanizing us, if they allow us to survive at all. Nevertheless, my view is also different from those who expect that our machines will allow us to achieve bliss. By the year 2076, I expect that the physical nature of our lives will not differ dramatically from today. Although advancing technology will allow us to explore new ways of living, many aspects of traditional lifestyles will remain as popular as ever. For example, we likely will still be preoccupied with Chippendale furniture and center-hall colonial homes. On the other hand, where I expect some of the biggest changes to take place is in the way that we communicate. In the year 2076 we will no longer grab at a ringing telephone or peer at a video screen for our electronic messages. We will not have to spend months of study to pick up a new language. We may even be able to learn from a dead relative why we were written out of her will. How exactly will we be using communication technologies to work, enjoy ourselves, maintain social networks, and, of course, annoy and impose on each other by the year 2076?

Master Trends

Before sketching a few specific ideas, I will posit a master trend. I foresee enormous progress in integrating electronic and auxiliary biological systems, particularly genetically engineered systems, with the human body. The input and output of those systems will be linked with the brain, and like our natural limbs and senses, they will meld seamlessly with our consciousness. In both the metaphorical and literal senses, people of the future will grow together with hardware systems as well as genetic and biological enhancements. Support for this trend can be found today. Surveys suggest that perhaps 10 percent of the U.S. population carry artificial devices (excluding simple devices like dental fillings and contact lenses) in their bodies.

Two hundred years ago, the trend was already under way, exemplified by the peg leg and George Washington's famous dentures. Modern devices include software-controlled heart pacemakers and artificial limbs that allow a proxy sense of touch. Increasing varieties of machines, such as cranially implanted electronic devices that give a measure of hearing to the deaf, are enhancing human capacity and functioning. Likewise, biological tissue from other species is being turned to our use. Medical researchers are actively investigating the transplantation of cells and organs from baboons, pigs, and other animals into human patients. From these steps the trajectories of progress will likely lead to biochemically or genetically manipulated and enhanced biological materials that are highly compatible with the human body. It could also lead to the ready integration of organs and tissues derived from other species, along with their specialized functions. We could, for instance, give ourselves a dog's sense of smell or a dolphin's sonar system. We would be fully conjoin—physically, neurologically, and operationally—with the biological resources of the animal kingdom, modified for our benefit.

Although many of us will welcome these advances, a vociferous minority will perceive such modifications as threats to our essential humanness, ontology, and teleology—with much justification. Others will object to the exploitation of animals for such purposes. These communities will only become further disturbed and energized as technological progress continues.

With the master trend in place, consider the way that we send a written message today. At some time in the past, we probably decided to buy stamps and stationery, then acted to acquire them, and finally set them aside for the present use. Now, as we sit at our desk, we think about the purpose of the message and decide on some questions. Will it be postcard or letter? Handwritten? Sent electronically? Mass mailing or individualized? We then prepare the message accordingly. Likewise, whenever we get our messages, be they from a mailbox, a computer, or a mobile phone, we make conscious decisions. In each case we process information and actuate ourselves at two levels: the conscious, mental level and the level of physical action. We plan our actions and then carry them out. The physical actions that we take often result in substantial commitments of time, energy, and money. We may stand in a post office line for an hour to send an overseas letter during holiday season or brave a snowstorm just to get to a mailbox. In awaiting email messages, many of us look in our in-boxes several times an hour, and when we expect an important message, we may waste time impatiently checking and fretting. In 2076 I expect that sending a message will involve exactly the same process of planning and acting, but it will all take place at the mental level. We will still decide when to compose a message and by what modality to send it—voice, video, or written, and whether it should be addressed individually or network-wide—but perhaps we can also decide if it will be symbolic or abstract, options that we can implement only clumsily today. If we want to send it in writing, we will compose it much as we do now on a computer screen, but the screen will be replaced by a mental image that we summon up. Rather than typing or speaking aloud to compose our missives, we will use mental dictation. In point of fact, numerous voice-recognition dictation programs today can write down our words with surprising (but less than perfect) accuracy.

These seeming tricks of mental legerdemain, although not easily attainable with today's technology, should not be as hard to achieve as they may first appear. Clearly, our speech is the physical embodiment of well-established mental routines. We think thoughts and say words; the saying is the neural activation of muscles in our voice box, mouth, and diaphragm. Nevertheless, we also can imagine saying things or can even say them silently. What needs to be done is to harness the neural impulses for these silent actions to biomechanically integrated devices, which would be linked to the communication network of the outside world. Our volition then would invoke these machines rather than our anatomy to send and receive messages. To check our email, or perhaps more accurately mind mail, we would first decide to look at it and then take actions to access, review, and respond to it. The major difference is that we only would have to activate our mind. Looking at our mind mail would be little different from the way we look at physical mail, except that we would view it literally through the mind's eye. After all, when we read a letter on a computer display, we experience phenomenologically the observation of physical words and letters.

Of course, all of this is mental interpretation of neurological phenomena. Our brain assembles a set of sensory signals into what appears to be a solid image. The point is that mentally perceived embodiments of a phenomenon may bear little relationship to the underlying physical reality. Recent achievements in brain research suggest that the technology of mind mail is entirely plausible. Noninvasive brain imaging techniques such as functional magnetic resonance imaging (fMRI) can distinguish between the thought patterns required for speaking and reading. Scientists have demonstrated that people can control the electroencephalograph (EEG) activity of their own brains. In turn, these EEG activities have been used to control computer functions, including cursor movement. Such achievements indicate that we have the nascent capability to compose and send messages using mental activity alone.

Telling Tales

Throughout history people have been killed in the hoary expectation that "dead men tell no tales." For this aphorism to remain valid in the year 2076, killers may have to be a great deal more thorough. As progress continues in our understanding of the biochemical underpinnings of brain function, I expect the appearance of a new "one-way" mode of communication—namely, from the dead to the living. I am not predicting a return to the séance as a form of evening entertainment, but rather that in a number of special cases, the biochemically stored memories of the dead will be available for inspection by the living. In one sense, this is not as unprecedented as it sounds and we have versions of it today. To illustrate, many people in anticipation of a time when they will be dead arrange to "send" messages to those who will be alive after them. These communiqués include letters, wills, videotapes, diaries, and monuments (Gumpert, 1987).

By the year 2076, however, even people who made no such prearrangements may be "speaking" to the living—their memories, experiences, and thoughts open for inspection. Similarly, people who are still alive but in the process of dying may also be candidates for this form of communication. As was demonstrated in 1998 by the "stained dress" incident in the investigation that preceded President

Bill Clinton's impeachment, extremely salient information can be adduced from the tiniest of biochemical traces. By means of forensic, pathological, archaeological, and anthropological investigations, researchers regularly gain immense insights from biochemical evidence. (The level of progress is that some investigators have called for the exhumation of the remains of Abraham Lincoln to determine whether had suffered from the hereditary disorder known as Marfan's syndrome.) Investigation of biochemical messages also extends to the residues of experiences—molecular markers—that are borne by the living.

According to a November 1998 report published in *New Scientist*, researchers pinpointed a biochemical signature, quinolinic acid, that in children can help differentiate brain injuries caused by accidents from injuries caused by violent abuse. Thus, even if babies cannot speak, they can tell a story. In 1991, tourists found a body protruding from the ice of an alpine glacier on the Italian-Austrian border. At first suspected to be a murder or accident victim of recent vintage, the body soon was shown to be the extraordinarily well-preserved remains of a 5,300-year old Stone Age man, nicknamed the Iceman. Numerous scientists subsequently examined the remains in intricate physical and chemical detail, seeking to glean insight into every aspect of the man's physical and social existence—where had he come from, what had he eaten and when, what technologies and skills had he possessed, what injuries and diseases had he suffered and at what age had he experienced them. Consider for a moment that on that cold glacier, as the Iceman approached death, he could have had no inkling of the extent to which his life and activities would be scrutinized, and by whom, five millennia later.

Might we suffer a similar fate? Could our secrets, experiences, and longings be pried from us after our deaths, if not millennia later then perhaps within seconds or minutes? A positive answer would seem to undermine our concept of the meaning of death. It is a common supposition in our culture that, when we die, our cognitive structure dies with us. In the year 2076, death may not be the end of us, at least as others know us. We might well be communicating details of our lives that we had believed would go with us to the grave. Many researchers suspect that our long-term memories are encoded in the chemical or electrochemical substrate of the brain, and that, when we remember, we are accessing those codes. Future technology may allow the codes to be accessible, at least momentarily, to others after we are dead, presuming that the brain tissue has been properly sustained. What could serve as the "decoder" for the memories of the deceased?

One possibility is an already existing "machine"—the human brain itself, which has been exquisitely engineered by evolution for that task. The development of external machinery for decoding memories may still be beyond us in 2076, but ultimately it might be possible to do so in such a way as to render thoughts and mental images viewable on an external monitor—or even through the mind's eye, by means of the mind-mail technology described above. Prospects for the success of such "mind reading" presumably would be highest for people who are only moments dead, when their tissues are intact and nearly viable. The memories of those who have ceased their mental functioning for more than a few minutes, however, could remain forever beyond our grasp. Nevertheless, how much richer would our historical insight now be if we could have plumbed the memories of, say, Lee Harvey Oswald on the cusp of death in order to know for ourselves what he knew about John F. Kennedy's assassination? If research in this area surges forward, more of us may be electing cremation after death. At the very least, new rights and legal guidelines would have to be established to deal with biological residues and the information that they contain. As intriguing as a trip down a dearly departed's memory lane might be, the prospects of similar mind reading among the living are far more awesome.

As mentioned earlier, using functional MRI (fMRI), scientists already can tell much about an individual's thought processes. Further instances beyond those enumerated above include when a person is reading a text or whether a person who is speaking a second, acquired language learned it before or after about the age of four. Doubtless this capacity to read the workings of the brain will grow. Consider how much more circumspect and tenuous our own lives would be if we knew that our innermost thinking or darkest deeds might be opened up for inspection, against our will. Imagine the chill that this might cast over the quality of interpersonal communication and internal reflection. More intriguing, perhaps, would be the ability not only to mind read but also to "mind feed." Mind-feeding technology, an obvious extension of the mind-reading variety, would allow us to enter extrinsic memories into our brain to the extent that they would be indistinguishable from our own memories.

A general observation about information-storage media is that, if a given medium can be read, it can also be recorded on, whether it be paper, magnetic tape, optical discs, or molecules like proteins and DNA. Once researchers know how to read the brain, they should be able to record within the brain as well. Obviously, implanted memories derived from a native speaker of French would be a great way to learn the language in ten minutes. We might also benefit from replacing memories of bad experiences—ranging from a boring dinner party to physical abuse or a painful accident—with more pleasant or positive memories. On the other hand, the potential danger would be staggering if some people were able to implant artificial memories without the recipient's awareness. We might be made to believe, falsely, that we owed someone a great deal of money. Worse, someone could rob a bank and give us the memory of having done the deed, and then pointing the police and lie detector experts in our direction. At the more extreme end of the spectrum, what might the consequences be if a normally fair-minded world leader were given selected memories? Should the technology of mind feeding be realized, society will have to grapple with a problem that makes efforts at the control of nuclear weapons seem like child's play.

Enduring Human Problems

For many, the compelling question is not what tools we might use to communicate in the future, but how such tools might affect our personal lives and society. Today's mobile telecommunication technology can serve as an exemplar of one phenomenological and social problem that will lead us to become less happy. Besieged with messages and information, heavy users often appear exhausted, harried, and confused rather than informed, exhilarated, and fulfilled. One such acquaintance, whose armory of devices included laptop, pager, cell phone, and an electronic organizer-secretary spoke in desperation of being overwhelmed.

Perhaps the problem is best highlighted by the inspirational shibboleth of those telecommunication researchers of the 1980s who sought to build a system that would allow us to "reach anybody, anywhere, at any time." Whereas engineers may have seen it as the ultimate embodiment of a "good thing," potential users saw it as undesirable. The prospect for most people—even telecommunication executives—of being reached by anybody at all (for instance, a telemarketer), at any time they chose (the middle of the night), anywhere (in bed) was disquieting, to say the least. And this disquiet has been compounded by locational monitoring capabilities of telecommunication networks. Detailed location information can be gathered real-time on anyone who posseses a mobile phone.

Obviously, screening and other moderating technologies will be required, no matter what the telecommunication systems of 2076 will be. Those systems will also require new social conventions that can only be achieved through mutual accommodation. We are (as we always have been) in the midst of social adjustment to our technological regimes. Today, our attention is often focused on controlling the use of telephone technologies and the Internet in environments—schools or workplaces, for example—where the competing realities that they provide are considered distracting or unproductive.

In schools, telephone communication with the outside world can be limited, as it has been done, by banning the use of mobile phones and restricting the number of public phones. In the workplace, however, solutions are less straightforward. As sociologist Paul Attewell has noted, those who are in low-status, low-pay, low-training-cost, high-turnover jobs, such as people on an assembly line, are heavily monitored; their access to telephones for personal use is quite restricted.

On the other hand, people in jobs involving high status, high pay, high training cost, and low turnover are also much less monitored and have ready access to telephones for personal use during work hours. In addition, with the onslaught of the Internet has come an added problem: the unauthorized use of the technology for viewing materials that the employing organization deems offensive or time wasting.

The complexity of this issue was vividly illustrated for me when for my research I interviewed the president of a global telecommunications company. As we talked in his office, I noticed stock ticker information crawling across the bottom of his computer screen. During a pause in the interview, he quickly swiveled his chair to get an update of the status of his pending trades. If this is how one of the most responsible and highly paid members of the organization behaves, one can only imagine the behavior of the employees below him.

One solution may be found not in ever-more panoptic control and monitoring technology but in a modification of our mores and interpretations. Japan's culture might set an example in this regard. When I lectured in that country a few years ago, my hosts warned me not to be concerned if some members of the audience closed their eyes and tilted their heads forward for protracted periods. Knowing of the long hours that the Japanese dedicate to their jobs and schoolwork, I thought perhaps that this behavior would be a sign of tiredness (or the unstated alternative, a lack of enthrallment with my remarks). Not at all, I was told emphatically. The audience members desired to be at one with the group. Their behavior would be a sign of respect; they would be trying to listen more carefully to my words. This explanation satisfied me, and I was pleased at the respect that so many members of the audience showed me. There was no loss of face on either side.

To deal with the problems of social interaction that new telecommunication technologies, such as perhaps something along the lines of the mind mail that I propose above, will create, we will have to summon into existence new regimes for social interaction and entirely new standards of etiquette. My experience in Japan encourages me to believe that we can formulate such behavioral guidelines in a way that will allow people to accomplish what they desire, personally and professionally, without inflicting excessive humiliations or indignities on those around them. However, the tendency is certainly to gravitate towards technological solutions since social engineering of consent is often sub-optimally effective.

Regarding the Future

Another area of speculation beyond the mere machinery of future telecommunication is the way in which that machinery will be used and regarded. My expectations for 2076 are straightforward. We will use telecommunication technology as we always have to conduct business, find information, and entertain ourselves; to seek and conduct human relationships on myriad levels; and to exploit, cheat, molest, and harm each other. Today's unwanted junk mail, telemarketing calls, and email spam will have their counterparts in tomorrow's mind mail, just as they had in yesterday's roadside hucksters and medicine shows. Machines also will substitute for people when we tire of, or become uncomfortable with, human company, although for some of us it will always be an unsatisfactory substitute. Others, as Sherry Turkle has learned in her studies of old people's homes, are already having them foisted upon them as ersatz companions.

It is important to realize that just as technology is not frozen and changeless, neither are human values and attitudes. Society continually adjusts and adapts, and what is one era's anathema is another's desiderata. Hence, we should be cautious in projecting our own values onto those who will come after us.

A good example, as it relates to communication technology, is the telephone answering machine. When this technology became widely available in the 1960s and 1970s, its use was decried. Those who called a friend or business associate and encountered an answering machine would often leave a vituperative denunciation of the rudeness and insensitivity of its owner. People intrepid enough to use the device took care to pad their recorded greetings with lengthy apologies. The answering machine was held up as the technological cutting edge of a society bent on dehumanization. According to my own research, 1987 was a turning point. In that year a majority of people in the U.S. no longer felt it rude to have a telephone answering machine; the view predominated that it was acceptable, or even desirable, to have one. Today, the device, or its voicemail equivalent, is seen as a great convenience, if not a necessity, to all concerned. In fact, in our hurry-up world, the value perception of the technology has been turned completely on its head. People who greet callers with long, mollifying recorded messages are chided for not getting to the point quickly, and a vast segment of the population now judges that those who do not have answering machines or voicemail services are thoughtless if not downright rude.

From the viewpoint of morals and manners, telephone answering machines (and to some extent, voicemail) have introduced a new dilemma. Because they are often used to screen incoming calls, they allow the user to judge whether a particular caller is worthy of attention in real time or sufficiently unimportant to be dealt with later, if at all. The situation is further complicated by the caller's suspicion that the person being called is present and available but not "picking up." Thus, the technology of the answering machine can be held accountable for a tangle of social intrigue that includes heightened distrust, suspected motives, hypersensitivity to nuances, and feigned unavailability. Such entanglements will grow even more byzantine as new communication technology becomes available.

In 2076, with potentially all manner of communication delivered directly into our minds and all our thoughts dispatched to others just as effortlessly, how can we fail to arrive at Nirvana? All bliss, at least all information and entertainment, will be available literally for the wishing—and, of course, the appropriate fee. This ultimate couch-potato existence will not come to pass in the next century, if ever. By nature, we like the company of others of our kind, and we enjoy full-fidelity experiences. Although it is feasible even now for many people never to leave the comfort and safety of their own homes, most of us like getting out and traveling at least some of the time. Indeed, the distance traveled annually by Americans grows year by year. Interestingly, in 1890 the average commute to work took twenty minutes. More than century later, after great advances in the technologies of mobility, untold billions of dollars invested in transportation infrastructure, and, more recently, the promotion of telecommuting and transit systems, the average commute to work hovers just a bit higher at about twenty-four minutes. This figures raises some intriguing questions about the way technology is used, or more correctly abused, to gain time trade-offs.

Being There

Today, with little effort, hundreds of millions of us can experience the great works of literature, art, and music. They are available through radio, television, audio and videotapes, compact discs, digital versatile discs (also called digital video disks), the Internet, and other modes of delivery. Nevertheless, despite such unprecedented electronic access, there seems to be little substitution effect; in-person attendance at museums, concerts, operas, plays, and exhibits continues to set new records. I would argue that the availability of electronic media stimulates rather than slackens interest in "being there." The explanation of this seeming paradox does not lie—as technology enthusiasts would have us believe—merely in the limited vividness of the electronic presentation. Rather, it stems from a singular factor: most people enjoy physical immersion in a social setting with other human beings. Furthermore, the benefits of such immersion itself are far from trivial. This last point may be demonstrated by reference to the behavior of sports fans. By means of clever electronic enhancements developed for sports coverage on television, a fan can get a hyper-realistic view of a home-team football game surrounded by all the domestic comforts, without having to pay for gas, negotiate traffic, or order tickets.

Nevertheless, sports stadiums show no sign of extinction but rather proliferate. The conveniences and features of television do not prevent tens of thousands of fans from crowding together in subfreezing temperatures to get a distant, single-perspective view of the game and paying lavishly in time, money, and energy for the privilege. Sports fans are by no means the exceptions. People of all ages pursue physical hardship and adventure. Mountain climbing, bungeecord jumping, paintball fights, and deer hunting are all popular (and occasionally lethal) activities. All have an element of danger and physical discomfort associated with them. None are in any sense necessary in our society. Social investment patterns are also interesting in this regard. Despite the emphases on telecommuting, distributed workplaces, and energy conservation, spending on highway construction is expanding. Although billions are spent on optical fiber for telecommunication, so too are billions spent on sports stadiums—what Joseph L. Bast, president of the Heartland Institute, has called "the pyramids of the twentieth century." Moreover, according to studies of the way that we invest our time, the hours whiled away on the Internet come at the expense of television watching rather than other activities. This suggests that there may be upper boundaries on the amount of time we are willing to invest in passive forms of entertainment. If, indeed, we are heading in the direction of technologically enabled physical stasis, we are not showing universal inclination to take advantage of it.

Future Freedoms

Perhaps the best way to look at the issue is in terms of problems and opportunities. As Edward Tenner (1996; 2003) has pointed our lives are made from our choices of technology, and we often reject what is possible or efficient for what is appealing or comfortable. Sometimes the lifestyle choices that we make are not as convenient as those that our forebears might have expected from us, given the anticipated advances in technology.

For example, in the early 1950s the magazine *Popular Mechanics* showed the future of life when most everything would be made of plastic. This miracle material of modern science not only would offer us a wide array of creative colors, but it also would allow the busy housewife to simply hose down the premises and dispense with dusting and mopping forever. We could have such houses today, but no one does.

The rage in the United States continues to be center-hall colonials, as anyone who has tried to sell their "modern" A-frame or Bauhaus-style home has discovered. There are more Doric and Ionic columns littering Europe, North America and Asia today than were ever built in ancient Greece and Rome. A fireplace can add $1,000 to a home's resale value, even if the home is buried deep in a city and far removed from the nearest forest. Some things simply appeal to us, regardless of their usefulness or modernity. In this sense, there is no technological determinism. Could the mind-mail and mind-reading technology that I foresee ultimately fulfill Lord Salisbury's nightmarish scenario envisioned for the telegraph, wherein people will "see everything that is done, and hear everything that is said"? Certainly the potential in us for such application is not lacking. We may wonder what further horrors the Soviet secret police or Nazi Gestapo would have perpetrated with the armamentaria of modern data-gathering and monitoring technology.

From those days of labor-intensive surveillance and paper records to today's computer databases, satellite tracking systems, and automated monitoring devices, it is but the same span of time that separates us from the future to which I refer. Pessimists justifiably bemoan the steady erosion of privacy by the government and commercial interests.

We have less privacy in many spheres than did our parents, but Americans and especially Europeans also have privacy-protection mechanisms that were not afforded prior generations. Powerful public key cryptography is available worldwide. Europeans enjoy strong juridical protections against illegal privacy invasions. In France, for instance, violators of privacy are liable to jail terms as high as five years. Those protections notwithstanding, the technology that can be marshaled against personal privacy is astounding. The array ranges from profiling and data-mining software systems to such hardware as infrared cameras that can see through clothing, "pinhole" video cameras that can be hidden in clocks or lamps, and spy satellites that can read the license plates of cars.

Even without the spectacular steps that may occur, our privacy and a wide selection of associated rights and freedoms might seem not only imperiled but on the way to annihilation. This is far from a foregone conclusion, however. Human society continually defies the pessimistic experts. Rather than extinguishing liberty and privacy, expanding interpersonal communication seems to be extending these treasured rights.

In recent years, communication technology has played a critical role in undermining totalitarian regimes in Eastern Europe and Latin America as noted in earlier chapters. By means of video recorders, fax machines, mobile phones, and the Internet, it is now easier than ever before to bring to public attention such reprehensible acts as police or domestic abuses, criminal and terror acts, genocide, and suppression of individual expression and to energize opposition forces. At the same time, I do not wish to minimize the widespread abuses that would be possible with advanced communication technologies. For instance, the potential technology of mind reading of the living and the dead could have terrible consequences for both the individual and the larger society. In the hands of criminals, totalitarian regimes, and even indifferent democratic governments, it could lead to massive invasion of privacy, involuntary extraction of information, and mental forms of plunder and rape.

As is the case with today's communication technologies, new technologies will require our extreme vigilance to control their harmful misuse. Technology is steered by human agency. The specific uses depend on the specific personalities involved. Predicting how technology will be used is inevitably surprising, as are its particular directions of development and the human needs that it will address (Tenner 2000). Orwell's dystopia was, after all, merely a future extrapolation of the appalling techniques and behavior that typified existing brands of totalitarianism. His predictions were entirely too plausible, and in presenting them in such a compelling way, Orwell bestowed upon us a grammar with which we can today fight the very evils he portrayed. Ironically, his dystopian vision has helped us avoid its realization.

Although issues of the destiny of human freedom are paramount, questions about human nature are also of profound interest. Looking over the millennia of recorded history, I am struck by the amazing consistency of human nature, by how little our drives and conduct have changed, by how powerfully the Greek tragedies and Shakespeare's plays still reach across the centuries to move us. Nevertheless, people and social norms do change, just enough in each new period of history to make the behavior of our forebears seem startling, or at least a little puzzling. Communication technology appears to be an important factor in this constant rearrangement and rebalancing of social processes. I am confident of one aspect of change: progress in technology in some way will alter cultural values and the quality of social interaction. Its effects will be such that, despite our smug certainty about our enlightened lifestyles and the correctness of our values, we assuredly will appear quite bizarre and opaque, if not utterly obtuse, to our great-grandchildren.

Note

This chapter is based on, Communication in the year 2075. *Science and the Future. Year 2000*. Annual Supplement of the *Encyclopedia Britannica*. Chicago and London: Encyclopedia Britannica, 2000, pp. 176-200.

References

Bellamy (1951 [1888]). *Looking backward*, 2000- 1887. New York: Modern Library.

Briggs, Asa (1989). *Victorian things*. Chicago: University of Chicago Press.

Czitrom, Daniel (1982). *Media and the American mind from Morse to McLuhan*. Chapel Hill, NC: University of North Carolina.

Gumpert, Gary (1987). *Talking tombstones and other tales of the media age*. New York: Oxford University Press.

Katz, James E. (1999). *Connections: Social and cultural studies of the telephone in American life*. New Brunswick, NJ: Transaction Publishers.

Kurzweil, Ray (1999). *The age of spiritual machines: When computers exceed human intelligence*. New York: Viking.

Moravec, Hans R. (1998). *Robot: Mere machine to transcendent mind*. New York: Oxford University Press.

Tenner, Edward (1996). *Why things bite back: Technology and the revenge of unintended consequences*. New York: Alfred A. Knopf.

Tenner, Edward (2000). "Future and Assumptions," Britannica Science and the Future. Year 2000. Annual Supplement of the *Encyclopedia Britannica*. Chicago and London: Encyclopedia Britannica.

Tenner, Edward (2003). *Our own devices: How technology remakes humanity*. New York: Vintage.

11

Concluding Thoughts

In this chapter, as in the previous one, I look forward based on an examination of the past developments. But in this essay, I do so less in the sense of technological potential and more in the sense of user needs and ways to assess them. I also review some major avenues where additional research and analysis are needed. The chapter ends by linking some of mankind's earliest cultural endeavors to those that continue today and in which mobile communication is playing an increasingly pivotal role.

The Future of a Futuristic Device

Some studies, including my own, find that part of the appeal of a mobile phone, especially for early adopters, is that it can seem like an artifact from the future. In a sense, the device allowed users to live at the edge of tomorrow. Having the latest and greatest may be part of the human competitive spirit, as described in chapter 3. Another aspect of the mobile phone's popularity was that it was a device that only elites could afford. It also meant that the user could command resources and deal with various contingencies. In essence, it bestowed power and became an iconic symbol of success and achievement.

So it is of little surprise that ads from the mobile phone's early days featured futuristic themes. Of course, utilitarian needs were also included in ad themes, especially that of safety and business efficacy. Yet from my inspection, the ads seemed to emphasize social connectivity and a vigorous, youthful fashion image. It generally took a bright, edgy, counter-domination theme. Fashion promotions and innovative design studios remain an important aspect of mobile phone conceptions and marketing initiatives. The parallels with cigarette ads are also intriguing, since both emphasize affordable luxury and take advantage of the rebellion and excitement that typifies youth.

Yet the forward-thinking, fashion-conscious approach is but part of the picture. As the mobile phone became more popular, and many segments of the population began adopting it, the mental image of the mobile phone, for many, began to change.

Certainly the futuristic tool image has remained important. But users themselves have begun adopting counter or even anti-uses and designs. Much attention was drawn to a small firm that was modifying old wireline phones and making them into mobile phones. And Pirjo Rautiainen has noted that punks and rockers in Sweden enjoy having clunky, out-of-date mobile phones. In this way, the young people can show that they are not part of the business-mobile phone ethos

A further illustration of the cultural, often retrograde, interpretation of mobile communication is the ringtone. Here personalization is extremely easy, relative to the change in the design of the phone itself. Although there are surveys of the most popular downloaded ringtones, and they have become a multi-billion dollar business, retrograde adoption is alive and well. Many people choose to have an old-fashioned jangling ringing bell of the 1950s era wireline sets. This observation illustrates the fact that constituencies of meaning do not universally endorse the futuristic image.

Fashion and anti-fashion are important dimensions. Numerous young people in the U.S., Korea, and Japan say that they are anxious to avoid appearing with a bulky mobile phone hanging from the front of their belts. To them, doing so would suggest that they had the same fashion sense as do old men who would typically wear their mobiles in the same position though with the belt cinched across their sternums instead of beneath their hips. Also to be avoided is the front breast pocket.

As compared to those of today, tomorrow's mobile users are likely to have quite different beliefs about the way the world is ordered, and the way it should work. The young generation's technical abilities continue to amaze older generations, as it has for generations. Multi-tasking is perhaps the most striking contemporary difference currently. Albeit, there are technologies that the old have mastered and about which the young have no understanding. A scene I witnessed illustrates this principle. Confronted for the first time with a fancy old "Empire"-style telephone, a ten-year-old boy was baffled about how to use it. This telephone had a rotary dial. Although the boy was bright, and knew how to download mobile phone games and ringtones, and was an adept denizen of online games and controllers, he was unsure about how to operate the rotary dial. How did one operate it? In effect, the mobile phone has been a de-skilling technology for him and a host of other young people. The efforts that AT&T went to in the 1930s to inculcate a generation of students in New York City about how to use the telephones of that era was, ultimately, in vain.

Both technology and terminology are becoming muddled. I witnessed this phenomenon in the following scene: an eight-year-old girl who was visiting her grandmother watched her fetch a bulky cordless phone to make a call. As the grandmother was getting ready to dial, she paused to inform the little girl that she, the grandmother, was first going to look up the telephone number in the phonebook. The little girl sounded surprised, and said, "Gee Grandma, does that phone of yours have a phonebook?" The little girl thought that the cordless phone had an internal phone book, just like mobile phones, a technology with which she was well acquainted. The little girl was surprised not by the possibility of an on-board phone book but rather that an old fashioned cordless phone could have an internal phone book (which it did not). The situation was all the more puzzling to the little girl because she actually did not know what a paper phone book was, having never seen one in use. Thus one of the great cultural and commercial icons of twentieth-century domestic life appears to be fast leaving the scene.

A lesson that may be drawn from these illustrations is that the traditional categories of twentieth-century tools are becoming, jumbled as mobile communication technology advances. The mobile phone is becoming, as suggested in earlier chapters, miniature homunculi of the person, holding not only one's access to the larger world but one's identity, self-knowledge, and future plans as well. A big and reasonable fear for many is the loss (or theft) of their mobile phone. Some have said they would be literally lost without it. It is something that is in a symbolic sense is a form of death. The mobile phone is becoming part of the users' brain, and its loss is a form of social amnesia.

Projecting Future Wants

Over the years, I have seen many researchers ask people to imagine a communication device they would like to have. When young people are asked to sketch the mobile phone they would like, they generally come up with incremental modifications of what is currently available. There are several possible explanations of this result; here I will summarize two of them. First, designers have done a great job of anticipating what users want, and that there is little chance that new designs could improve the human engineering aspects of the mobile phone's design. In other words, users are quite happy with what is available, and would want only a few tweaks. A second possible explanation, and one that I favor, is that it is difficult for non-experts to conceive of the possibilities of what could be done, and therefore there is a failure of imagination. Both explanations reveal a blindspot that often plagues market research.

Perhaps the situation can best be understood by offering a hypothetical illustration. If in 1880 a farmer were asked what solution he might prefer for a massive boulder in the middle of his field, he might speak of having a plow with a more flexible blade to help him get around the boulder more easily. It is unlikely that he would ask for a steam shovel or bulldozer to move the boulder out of his field altogether because of his unfamiliarity with near-term technological developments. And his response would sub-optimize any "market research" guidance being given to the designers of new systems. So the inability to articulate an optimal solution means that user wishes are at best an incomplete guide.

Still, focus groups no less than engineering imagination remain an important source for product innovation. With increasing ease of design and marketing of new phones, numerous different styles and approaches can be readily evaluated. Some will fail, of course, and others may turn out to be surprising successes.

At the same time, it has been said often enough that users do not want choices; they "want what they want." This shibboleth is correct up to a point. Not readily understood in such a formulation is that having too many choices actually leads to frustration. Part of the reason is because learning how to manage these choices is a cognitive burden. But even more importantly, unyielding psychological processes take place when humans are confronted with large numbers of choices. Generally speaking, the more choices people have, the less satisfied they are with any particular choice.

What does seem to be clear is that style no less than function is an important force acting on the evolution of mobile phone capabilities and market successes. Second, there is enormous desire to integrate comfortably the affordances of mobile communication and entertainment into the natural routines of the body in space. The earpiece allows the user to avoid having to hold the mobile up against the head even as it makes it difficult for those around the user to detect whether they are "in-frame" (subject of communication of the user) or out of frame (intentionally or unintentionally excluded from the communication). Certainly it seems that users are willing to sacrifice considerations about the comity and civility of public space in order to indulge their own private pleasures of personal communication. Again, this is evident when users on the street use in-the-ear speakers to ramble on loudly while they amble forward assertively. Their shouting of "hello" or "what do you want" confuses fellow pedestrians who may be a few feet ahead of them.

The difficulty of knowing where the audience fits in the mind of the user has given rise to decoy behaviors, in which the user pretends to be talking on the mobile phone, when in fact the "talking" is for the benefit of the audience. In this way, mobile phone users have raised their handsets to their heads to avoid having to talk to people they know, or increase their feelings of safety while navigating a parking lot at night. This example, drawn from chapter 1, demonstrates the proliferation of novel uses of mobile phones and the unintentional consequences of new technology.

All these factors make it difficult to predict future demands. Yet when one looks to the future to consider what devices might look like, and how people might use them, there are several sources of inspiration. Market professionals can look to the current crop of technologically advanced users, often gathering them in focus groups to discuss potential projects. Other times, Delphi methods drawing on experts have been employed. These can be helpful sources. Nonetheless, it is also important to consider the limitations of these sources. One reason is that, over the short-term, people suffer from a lack of imagination. Another is that what people advance as reasonable explanations and views aired during such exercises are often designed to create an impression or please the questioner.

Another limitation is that possibilities that are considered tend to be derived from one's local culture. This also leads to a failure of imagination. What people like does not necessarily spring from some need that can be articulated in advance and resolved via human factor engineering and new service offerings. Granted, usages cannot grow independent of human anatomy and cognitive abilities. But it is also well to recall the wide array of human decoration and enhancements, which range from lip stretching and tattooing to collagen injections and hair dying. It is also well to consider variation in human ritual, which for example can insist that some foods must be eaten and others must not, or at its most extreme, who shall live and who shall die. Hence, what people would want in their future communication devices depends on social circumstances that are yet to be defined. On the other hand, savvy marketing practices can create a technology that fits with the unfolding design Zeitgeist.

In general, though, we can identify several trends emerging for what future users will want in their communication devices. Tomorrow's devices that are likely to succeed will have to fit in with, or at least not be a symbol against, basic values and identities of the particular sub-subculture of users. Of course, one person's reference group or subculture is another person's anathema. Second, concerns about manners or public civility are unlikely to hinder long the adoption and use of an otherwise desirable technology. Despite public railing against use of mobile phones in the presence of others or doing email during meetings, over the reasonably short-term, nearly all moral barriers to their usage have collapsed. Without externally imposed sanctions, funerals, end-of-life discussion, and marriage ceremonies will soon be fair game for the mobile device consumer. Third, ease-of-use, including conformance with body actions, will also be important. In two words, people like comfort and convenience, and are willing to go to considerable lengths to obtain these attributes in their technology. Finally, qualities of "social applications" are going to be paramount. Devices will need to fulfill intelligently the users' social needs by helping them stay in contact with those who are socially meaningful while helping them avoid those who are boring or socially pernicious. (To paraphrase one acerbic newspaper editor in pre-*Anschluss* Vienna: there are people who want to kill me because of my opinions and there are those who want to spend time with me sharing their views. The police will protect me from the former!) To the extent a mobile device can achieve the ends outlined above, and help create new needs in these domains, then it will succeed.

Meaning of Time, Self, and Life-Space

An intriguing question that has captured the attention of researchers is how people understand the process of time and its change (Zerubavel 2003). Understandably, the question of how mobile communication technology is affecting people's understanding and use of time is paramount. It may be the case, for example, that the experience of one's day changes as a result of mobile communication; this would include subjective perceptions of time, its passage, and its meaning.

One phenomenological aspect might be what Ling and Yttri (2002) have dubbed "hyper-coordination," the sense that every moment is caught in a web of planning and interaction with others, and that plans can be changed quickly in light of circumstances and the actions of others. They also assert that mobile phones serve to soften one's sense of time. To put it differently, users of mobile phones appear to be more relaxed about redoing schedules and altering plans if they are able to use the mobile phone to coordinate with others.

It is even claimed, presumably hyperbolically, that the idea of being late may disappear altogether. Although such claims are extreme, it certainly seems subjectively that schedules can be negotiated more readily if there are changing circumstances, or even if internal subjective feelings change. Several studies reach this conclusion (Zernicke 2003), and it has even been suggested that "cell phones let us turn being late into being on time" (*Reader's Digest*, 2004). By this it is meant that by calling to a waiting party that one will be late in meeting them they then can (with the proper excuse) redefine the appointment time to a later one. The essential claim is that it is now more acceptable to all parties involved to adjust social and business schedules. This certainly is the conclusion that Rheingold (2002) reached on the basis of having talked about this issue with mobile phone-using teenagers in Tokyo.

Related to this topic is whether it is the case that mobile phones seem to fragment and isolate the self. Some researchers have focused on how mobiles reduce people's self-reliance, which in turn erodes their ability to react adaptively to unpredictable encounters.

Geser (2003) for instance claims that mobile phones can blunt the development of certain social competencies. This is because of the constant availability of external communication partners (as sources of opinion and advice) as mobile phones enable people to retain primary social relationships over distance. This affects people's self-reliance, making them unable to operate alone and leaving them dependent on the mobile as a source of assistance and advice. Witness, for example, increasing numbers of people using their mobile phones while shopping in grocery stores or video rental shops, asking their family or partners what they should get.

In terms of the mobile phone as the device for filling unoccupied stretches of time, many have expressed concerns about how the mobile phone is used to avoid being alone with one's thoughts. In Japan, the traditional ways of killing time (e.g., reading books, comics, newspapers) are losing out to mobile phones. Fortunati (2002) shows how the use of the mobile has encouraged more productive use of time. There can be little doubt that time spent commuting, waiting in queues at banks and airports—time ordinarily considered wasted—can now be used to communicate with others via the mobile phone.

Among the analysts who have considered how the mobile phone is altering one's life-space are Peters and Hulme (2002). In their view, the mobile phone is seen by users as an extension of their self. By the same token, the loss of a mobile phone is felt not just on the material level but also on the level of one's sense of physical self. Indeed, some even see such a loss as the psychological equivalent of physical disintegration. Should a person leave home without the mobile phone, that person may have a definite sense that something is missing and will often return home to fetch it. "A human with a mobile in the pocket is appreciably different from the human without one" (Moseley, 2002: p. 37).

The mobile phone seems to be altering in a rather profound way the ordinary structure of everyday life.

Invitation to Further Exploration

Many other research topics are worthy of further investigation. A small sampling is offered here to suggest the range of issues that mobile communication is posing for us. Put in highly abbreviated form, they include:

- What does it mean to be "with someone" also on a mobile. How does the splitting of attention between present and distant locations affect respective social relationships? Could we be hollowing out our social relationships, or building, as Ling (2004) suggests, walled gardens around our social selves?
- Are we moving from a phenomenology of writing to one of image, as Nyiri (2004) argues?
- Are there going to be more semi-spontaneous and coordinated group activities in the public sphere? Will the modes of initiating contact for social relationship creation be modified as a result of this technology?
- Will the practice of democracy change as a result of the availability of mobile communication technology and new modes of information dissemination and social organization?
- How will international crime control and anti-terrorism efforts be affected by mobile communication? Already both the conduct of terror and efforts to safeguard people's lives are being affected by mobile communication, but who is gaining an advantage and with what results?
- Are there net benefits from the constant "perpetual contact" that people are increasingly experiences due to their organizational involvement?
- How will peer-to-peer mobile communication technology affect institutions?
- Will mobile communication technology serve to dessicate local commercial life as automatic and "self-service" and "do it yourself" approaches erase the retail and middle management classes? What will the experience of shopping be like when the clerks and petite-bourgeoisie are replaced self-service systems? How will this affect urban and suburban landscapes and social life? Will a "mobile divide" be created, especially to the disadvantage of the non-mobile elderly and already socially marginalized?
- How are users and service providers re-configuring social relationships from proliferating mobile communication functionalities? To what extent are these new services created by users?
- How adequate are contemporary social science theories for understanding mobile communication behavior and human meaning-making? Are they in need of revision or supersession?

These issues are posed in the form of rhetorical questions. To investigate them thoroughly, they must be broken down into further components for detailed analysis. It may also be the case that it will be difficult to gather good data on them. Yet despite these considerations, the answers to them will be quite important.

Coda

A major theme of this book has been the role played by mobile and information technology relative to enduring patterns of human behavior and thoughtways. This theme was particularly focused on human-meaning making processes, especially related to identify, affect, and transcendence. As one might expect, some traditional aspects of these patterns have become diminished due to widespread use of communication technology. Nonetheless, there have been some surprising instances where the technology has had the opposite effect, helping strengthen patterns that are in many ways the opposite of modernism. Moreover, despite the critical theoretical assertions to the contrary, the technologies themselves get remade and customized by users, creating yet new patterns and applications. Some of these even subvert the goals of the designers of the original technology systems.

In closing, I would like to highlight a pattern of technologically enhanced cultural communication, which includes fashion and transcendence, that may be as typical of our forebears as it is today. This may be seen when Professor Christopher Henshilwood (University of Bergen) uncovered in South Africa what appears to be the oldest known jewelry—75,000-year-old pierced and ocher-tinted tick shells (*Nassarius kraussianus*). His discovery in 2004 suggested the importance of jewelry and other forms of decorative symbols interpersonal communication and representation. Henshilwood asserts that "once symbolically mediated behavior was adopted by our ancestors it meant communication strategies rapidly shifted, leading to the transmission of individual and widely shared cultural values" (Graham, 2004). If we agree with Professor Henshilwood's assessment of the import of the initial use of symbolic display technologies (in this case, tick shell decorative jewelry), the implications for evolving practices of mobile communication technology may be even more significant than we generally assume. Specifically, novel forms of widespread mediated communication could alter the cultural values we embrace and transmit. They could also transform social structure, interpersonal processes, and use of public space in ways we might neither anticipate nor desire. Yet through the thousands of years, the emotional, spiritual, and transcendental connotations that humans assign to their material world seem to endure. Personal decoration has long been used to identify publicly and confirm introspectively one's role, responsibility, and goals. This would seem to be the case for the mobile communication device no less than the pharaoh's nemes headdress or the tick shell. In fact, it is notable that both seashells and pearls remain important objects of personal decoration and status reflection and their inclusion on mobile devices complements, not replaces, such displays.

A recurring argument of this volume has been that mobile devices extend and enrich, rather than supplant, identity creation and displays already underway through other processes and items. This argument is also extended to the larger meaning-making in which people engage as a lifelong process. Conquest of the gene, the atom, and molecular chemistry appears to have touched but little the spiritual life that most people lead. The power of empirical research—demonstrated through advanced technological applications—is not interpreted by most as vindication of the scientific methods. Rather, the fruits of rational analysis are applied not to banishing the mystical world of the spirit but to further embellish them. Paradoxically, the very technologies enabled by empiricism and skepticism are used to advance mindsets that are often hostile to science and technology. A central aim of the eighteenth-century Enlightenment thinkers was to free humanity from superstition and other forms of what they saw as human intellectual enslavement. The fruits of this movement are responsible for the creation of the advanced telecommunication infrastructure that has given rise to the mobile phone and other mobile devices. An important purpose of these devices is not only to achieve utilitarian purposes ranging from emergency communication to commercial activities to entertainment. It is also used to create and sustain human relationships. And as demonstrated in this volume, they are also used to convey values and seek meaning. In fact, it may be the case that the very achievements of material success, far from quenching the human thirst for spiritual fulfillment heightens it. As science steals secrets, and with it nominal control of the ordered universe, and from myth, religion and tradition, life as experienced by many becomes drained of the magic that sustains the human creature, or so it seems to them. In the face of this onslaught, mobile devices can reclaim and probe the world of sentiment and mysteries. The technology enables people to search for new paths of spiritual control and fulfillment.

Powerful indeed is the need of humans to search for meaning that purportedly lies beyond the material horizons of ordinary existence. Mobile technology seems ideally suited to search for dimensions beyond the human ken. Human devices diffuse the magic of the human imagination into the air; from there it can be recaptured and harnessed for the pursuit of personal meaning.

Note

This chapter is based on, The next phase of research on mobiles. Workshop presentation, "Mobile communications and a culture of thumbs," MCM Institute/Sankt Gallen University, British Museum, London, July 20, 2004.

References

Brownfield, Paul (2004). Lack of cell phone etiquette draws ire. *Los Angeles Times*, April 24. Retrieved from http://www.centredaily.com/mld/centredaily/living/8510620.htm?template=contentModules/printstory.jsp.

Fortunati, Leopoldina (2002). Italy: Stereotypes, true and false. In James E. Katz and Mark A. Aakhus (Eds.), Perpetual contact: Mobile communication, private talk, public performance. New York: Cambridge University Press, pp. 42-62.

Geser, Hans (2003). Towards a sociological theory of the mobile phone. Release 2.1. September. Retrieved from http://socio.ch/mobile/t_geserl.htm#8

Graham, Sara (2004). Ancient shells may be earliest jewels. April 15. Scientific American.com. Retrieved from http://www.sciam.com/article.cfm?articleID=000084C2-188C-107F-988C83414B7F0000&sc=I100322.

Haddon, Leslie (2004). Information and communication technologies in everyday life. A concise introduction and research guide. London: Berg.

Ilkonetel (2004). "Islamic mobile phone launched." Retrieved from http://www.ilkonetel.com/UAE-Press.html.

Katz, James E. (1999). Connections: Social and cultural studies of the telephone in American Life. New Brunswick, NJ: Transaction Publishers.

Katz, James E. (2004). A nation of ghosts? Choreography of mobile communication in public spaces. In Kristof Nyiri (Ed.), Mobile Democracy: Essays on Society, Self and Politics. Vienna: Passagen Verlag, pp. 21-32.

Katz, James E. and Mark Aakhus (2002). Apparatgeist. In James E. Katz and Mark A. Aakhus (Eds.), Perpetual contact: Mobile communication, private talk, public performance. New York: Cambridge University Press, pp. 287-317.

Ling, Richard S. (2004). Mobile connection: The cell phone's impact on society. San Francisco, CA: Morgan Kaufmann.

Ling, Richard S. and Birgitte Yttri (2002). Hyper-coordination via mobile phone in Norway. In James E. Katz and Mark A. Aakhus (Eds.), Perpetual contact: Mobile communication, private talk, public performance. New York: Cambridge University Press, pp. 129-59.

Morris, Desmond (1977). Manwatching: A field guide to human behavior. New York: Harry N. Abrams.

Moseley, L. (2002). Digital culture: Rise of the thumb kids. Newsweek, May 6, 37-38.

Nyiri, Kristof (2004). Pictorial meaning and mobile communication. In Kristof Nyiri (Ed.), Mobile democracy: Essays on society, self and politics. Vienna: Passagen Verlag, pp. 157-184.

Reader's Digest (2004). Only in America. Reader's Digest (April), p. 19.

Rheingold, Howard (2002). Smart mobs: The next social revolution. Cambridge: Perseus.

Textually.org (2004). "Phones have been blessed in a ritual at a Matsu temple" July 1. Retrieved from http://www.textually.org/textually/archives/004381.htm

Zernicke, Kate (2003). Calling in late. New York Times, October 26, section 9, pages ST1, ST11.

Zerubavel, Evitar (2003). Time maps: Collective memory and the shape of the past. Chicago: University of Chicago Press.

Index